Earth Dwellers: Fish And Creatures In Water Coloring Book For Adults

By

R. L. Gemeinhardt

Other Books by R. L. Gemeinhardt available from Amazon.com

- Earth Dwellers Guide To Recycling And Environmental Conservation For Kids And Teachers
- Earth Dwellers Guide To Recycling And Environmental Conservation For Companies
- Earth Dwellers Guide To Recycling And Environmental Conservation
- Earth Dwellers: Birds And Animals Coloring Book For Adults
- Earth Dwellers: Boats, Docks, And Beaches Coloring Book For Adults
- Earth Dwellers: Our World Outside And Nature Coloring Book For Adults
- Earth Dwellers: Mountains , Rivers, Trees, Flowers Coloring Book For Adults
- Earth Dwellers: Mountains , Fish And Creatures In Water Coloring Book For Adults

- Making A Stock And Other Activities For A Healthy Life And Save The Planet At The Same Time
- Easy Company Recycling And Energy Saving Activities That Can Also Save Money
- A CLICHÉ A DAY
- Kids Activities To Help Save The Planet
- Sustainability Activities We All Can Do To Help Save The Planet

- DEMOB THIS!!! A Jack Owens novel as he responds to the spill from hell!

- Texas Used Oil Management: A Practical Guide To Compliance
- Used Oil Federal Regulations Management: A Used Oil Handler Guide For Environmental Compliance

AUTHOR WEBSITE: RLGEMEINHARDT.COM
Author Email - rlgemeinhardt@gmail.com

COPYRIGHT & CREDITS

Text copyright © 2021 R. L. Gemeinhardt.
Cover art copyright © 2021 R. L. Gemeinhardt.
All rights reserved.

No part of this publication may be reproduced, distributed, or transmitted in any form or by any means, including photocopying, recording, or other electronic or mechanical methods, without the written permission of the copyright owner, except in the case of brief quotations embodied in reviews and certain other non-commercial uses permitted by copyright law.

Requests for authorization should be addressed to VRM Group, LLC
Attn: Ron Gemeinhardt
918 Boxelder Pointe
League City, TX 77573

ISBN: 9798732293289

Limit of Liability/Disclaimer of Warranty: While the publisher and author have used their best efforts in the publication of this work, neither author nor publisher makes any representations or warranties with respect to the accuracy or completeness of the contents of this work and specifically dis- claim any implied warranties of merchantability of fitness for a particular purpose. No warranty may be created or extended by sales representatives or written sales materials. The advice and strategies contained herein may not be suitable for your situation. You should consult with a professional where appropriate. Neither the publisher, nor the author shall be liable for any loss of profit or any other commercial or personal damages, including but not limited to special, incidental, consequential, or other damages.
☐

This is the Coloring Book for any Earth Dweller wanting to relax and get some stress out of their lives and focus on the joy of coloring, in markers, crayons or even water colors it is all up to you.

Each page line drawing has the photo on the next page of the line drawing it was based on giving you a guide as to the gray color scheme but you would probably want to improve on it, please feel free to do just that. Unfortunately, if I provided the color photo the book would be more than twice the cost do to printing cost. But if you really want the color photo of a particular coloring book page I will send up to 5 of them to you via return email FOR FREE. But you will need to do the following: Put the book title in the subject line with the words REQUEST FOR PHOTOS and SEND ME A PICTURE OF YOU HOLDING YOUR COPY OF THE BOOK (I DON'T NEED TO SEE YOUR FACE OR BODY IF YOU DON'T WANT TO - I WILL DELETE ALL EMAILS AFTER I SEND YOU BACK YOUR PHOTOS - I WILL KEEP YOUR EMAIL ADDRESS FOR REFERENCE AS TO NUMBER OF REQUESTS AND PUT IT ON MY EMAIL LIST. With your photo holding the book enter the page numbers of the of the photo you want starting from the Title Page as page 1 in the body of the message. Send your EMAIL to rgemeinhardt@yaho.com and I will send you the color version (a few are only black and white but only about 10 in all the books) in about a week. If you really want them all then send a check for $5 USD to the address above with your email and I will send them all back to you via the email you provide. Please remember you are only allowed One free group if 5 per email for each book

Now what is left is just to pick one and go for it!!!

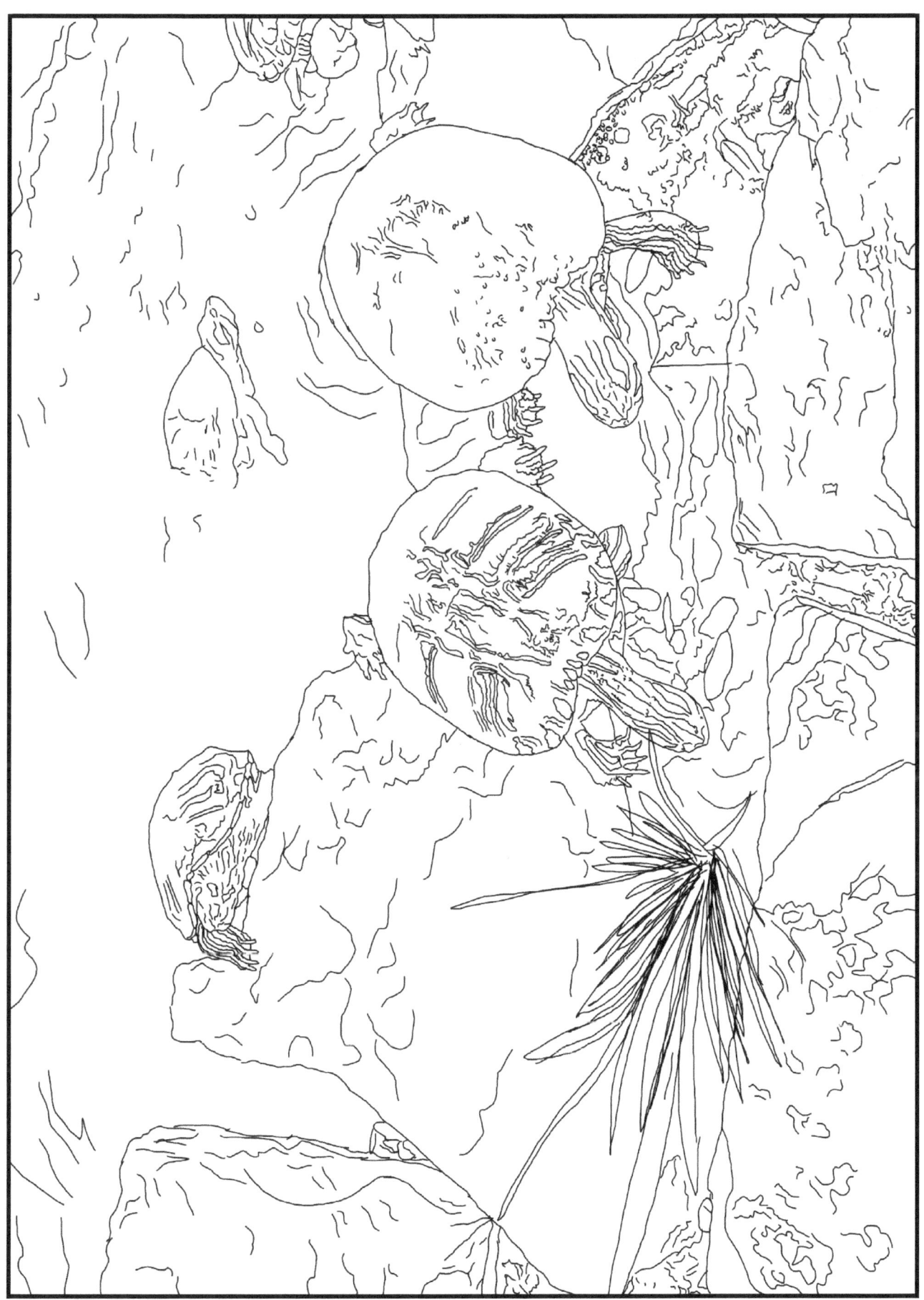

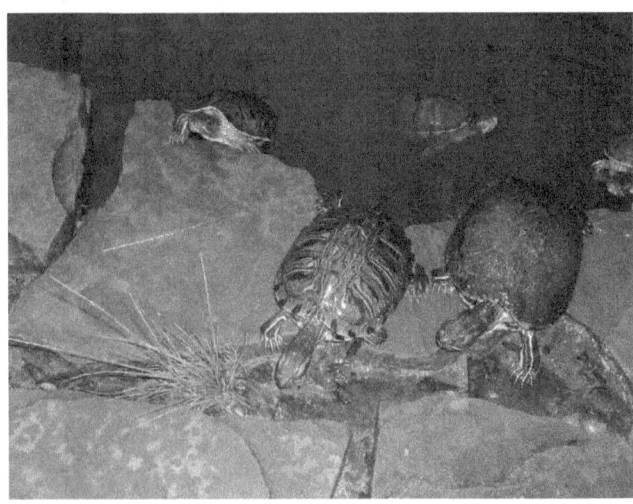

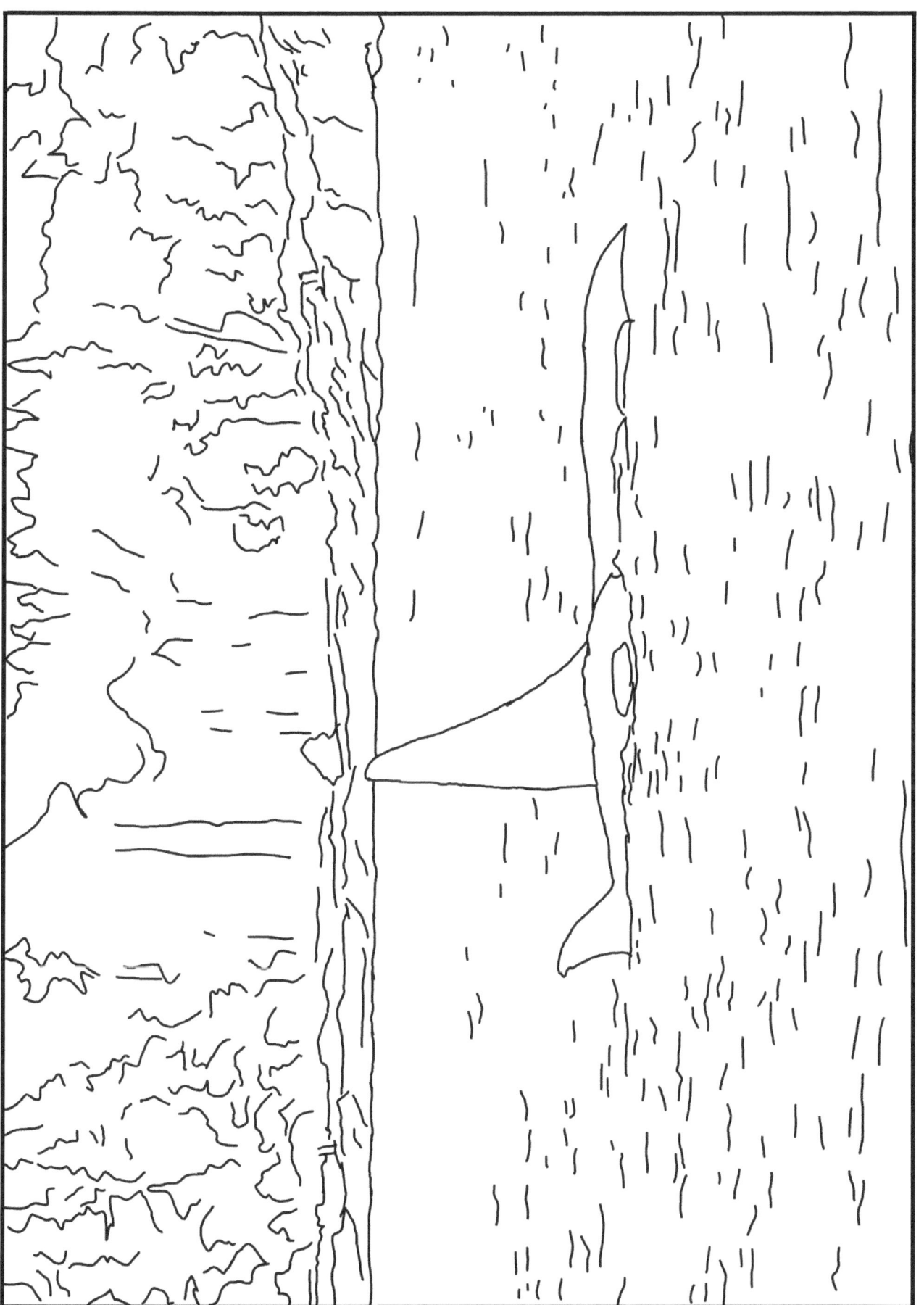

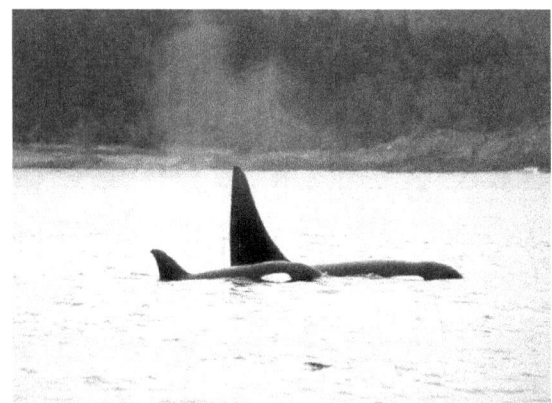

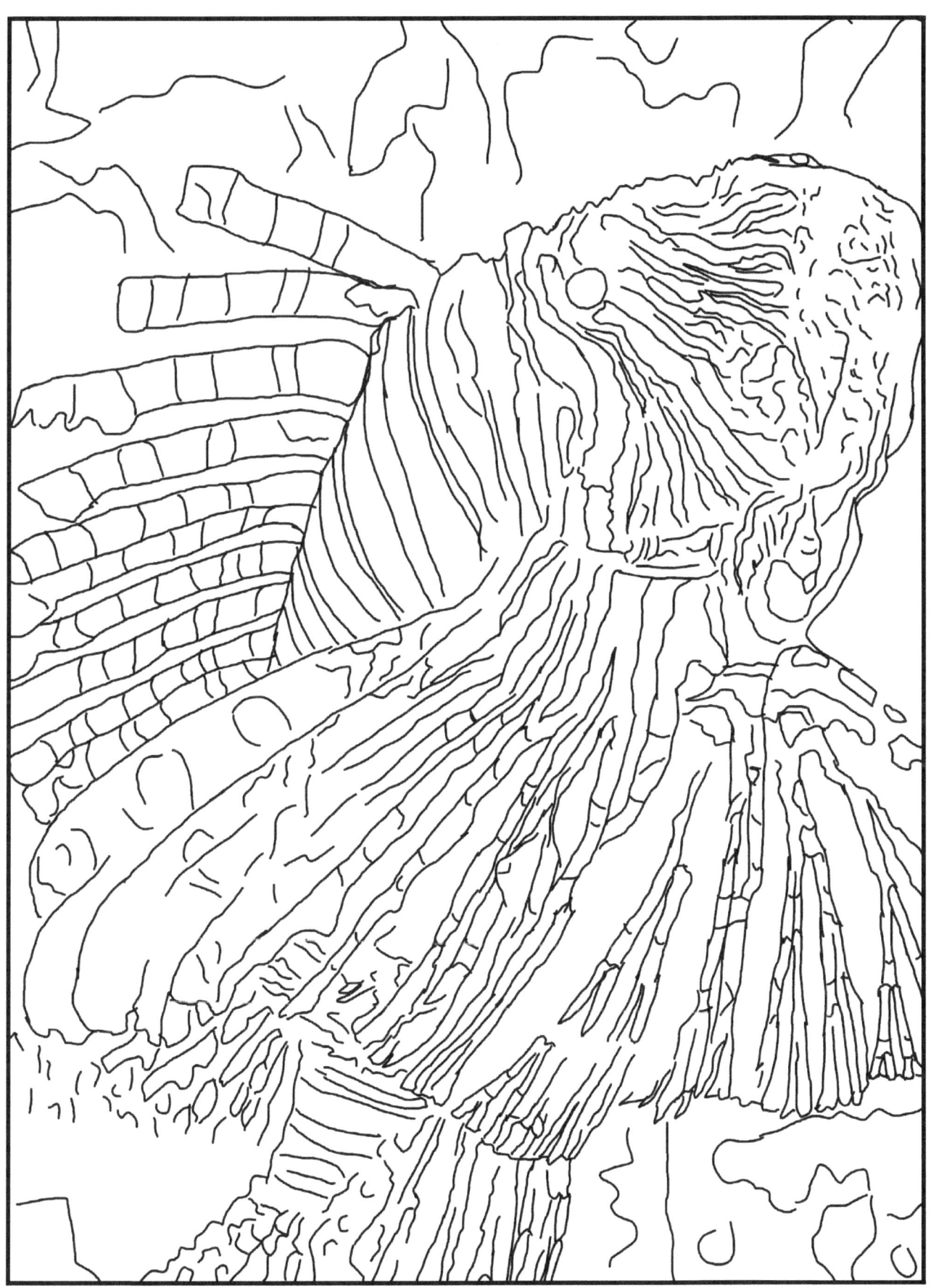

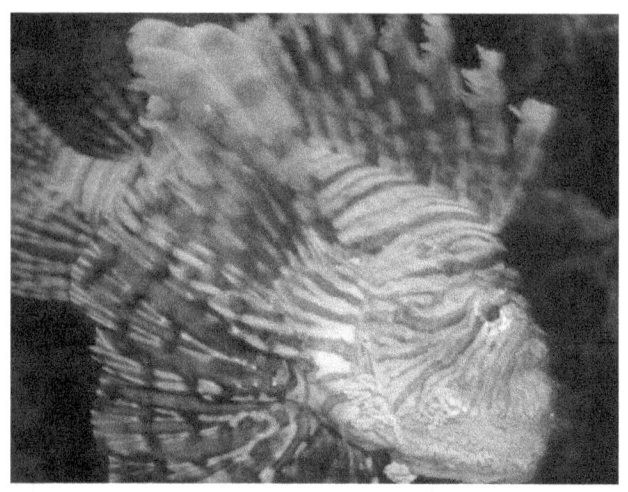

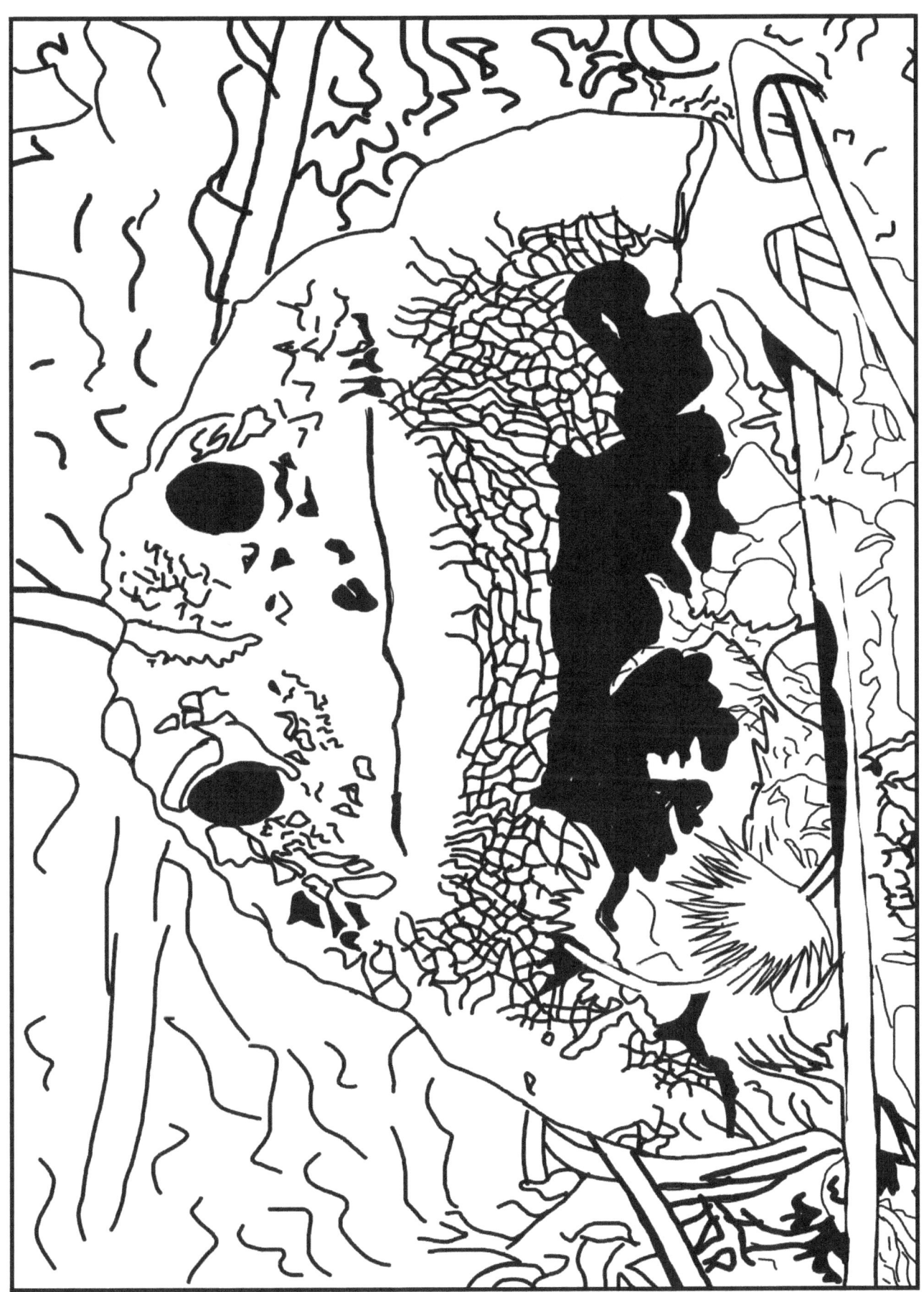

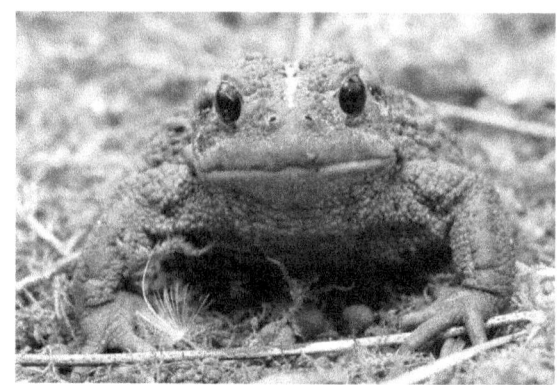

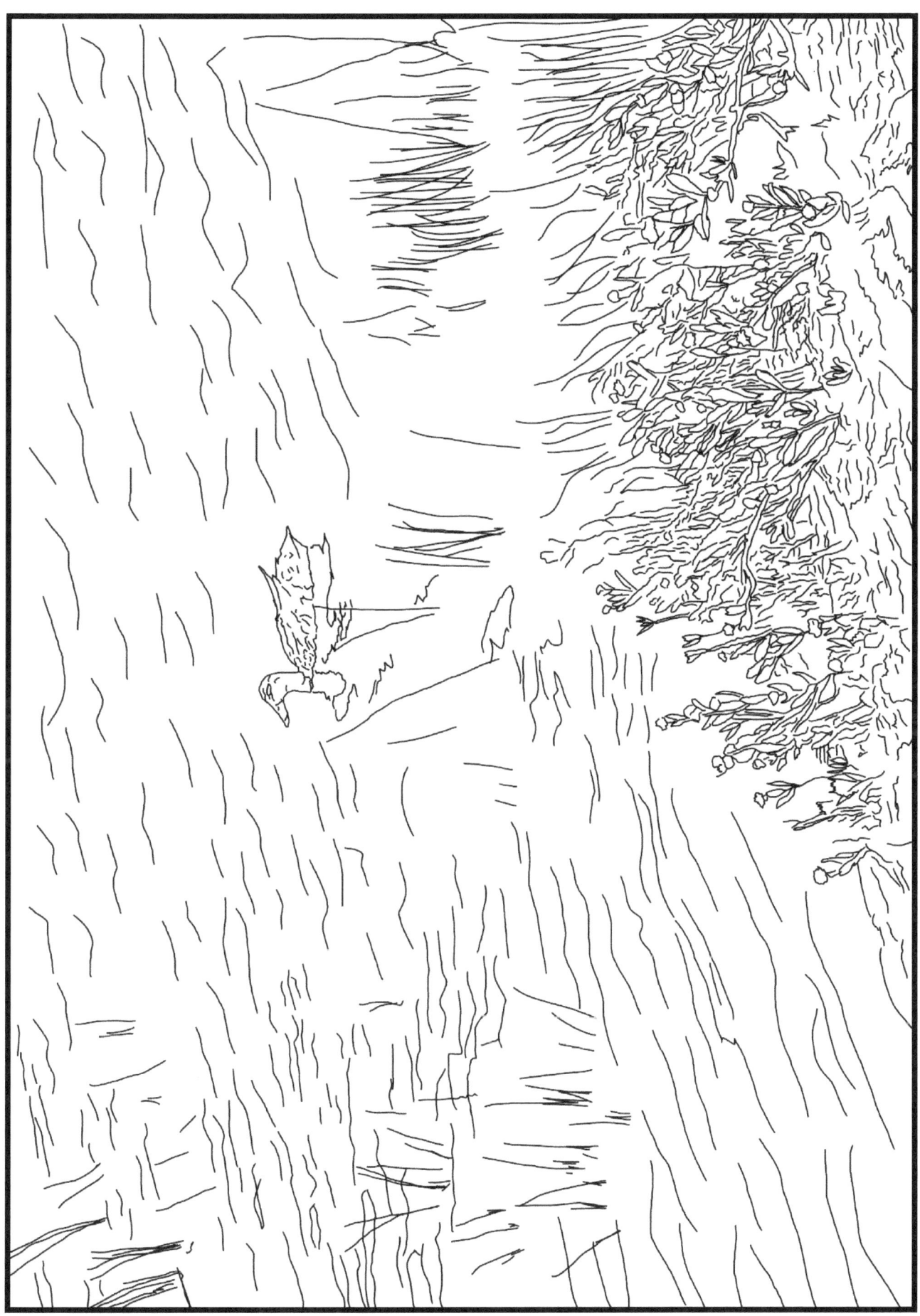

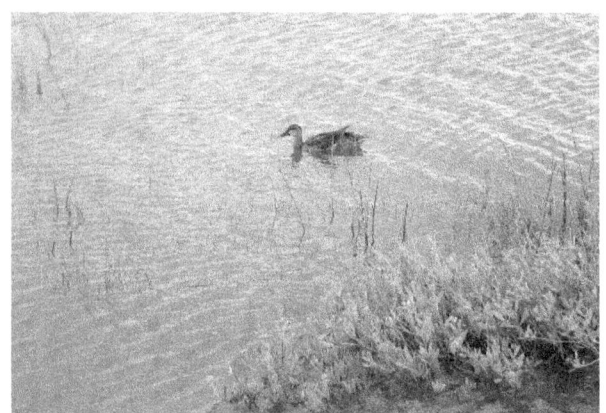

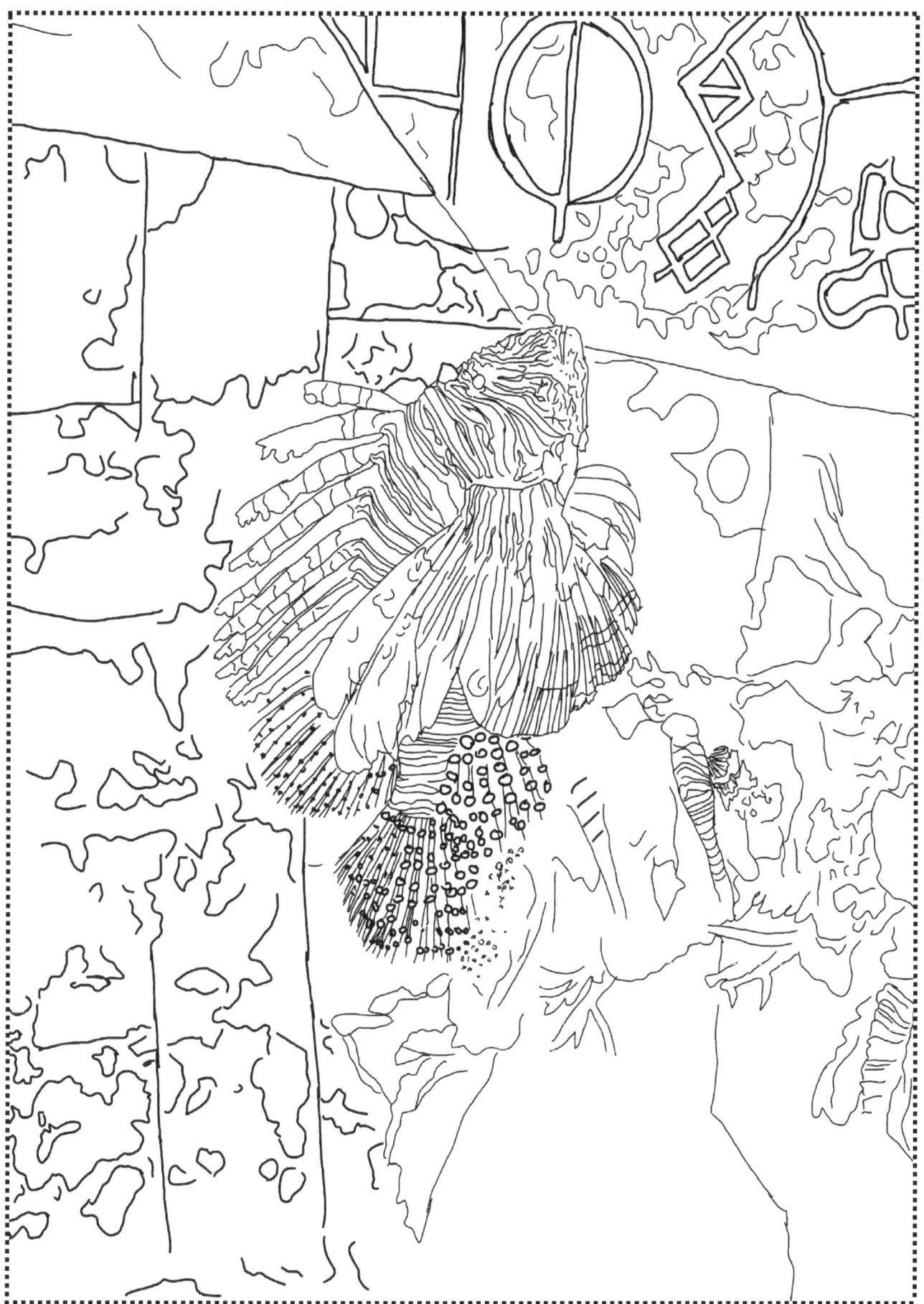

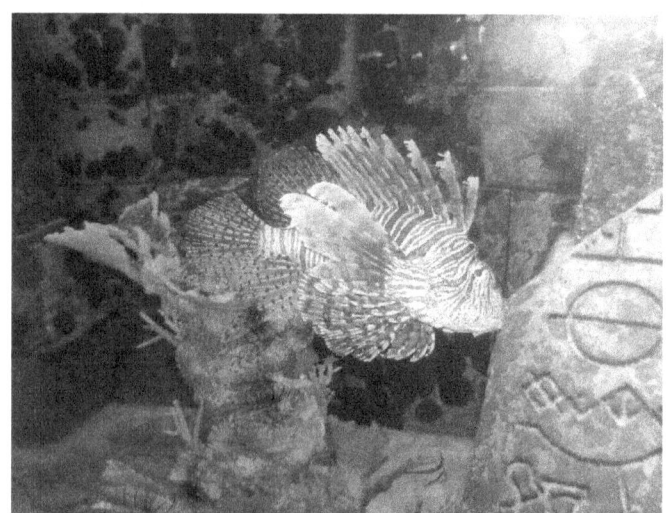

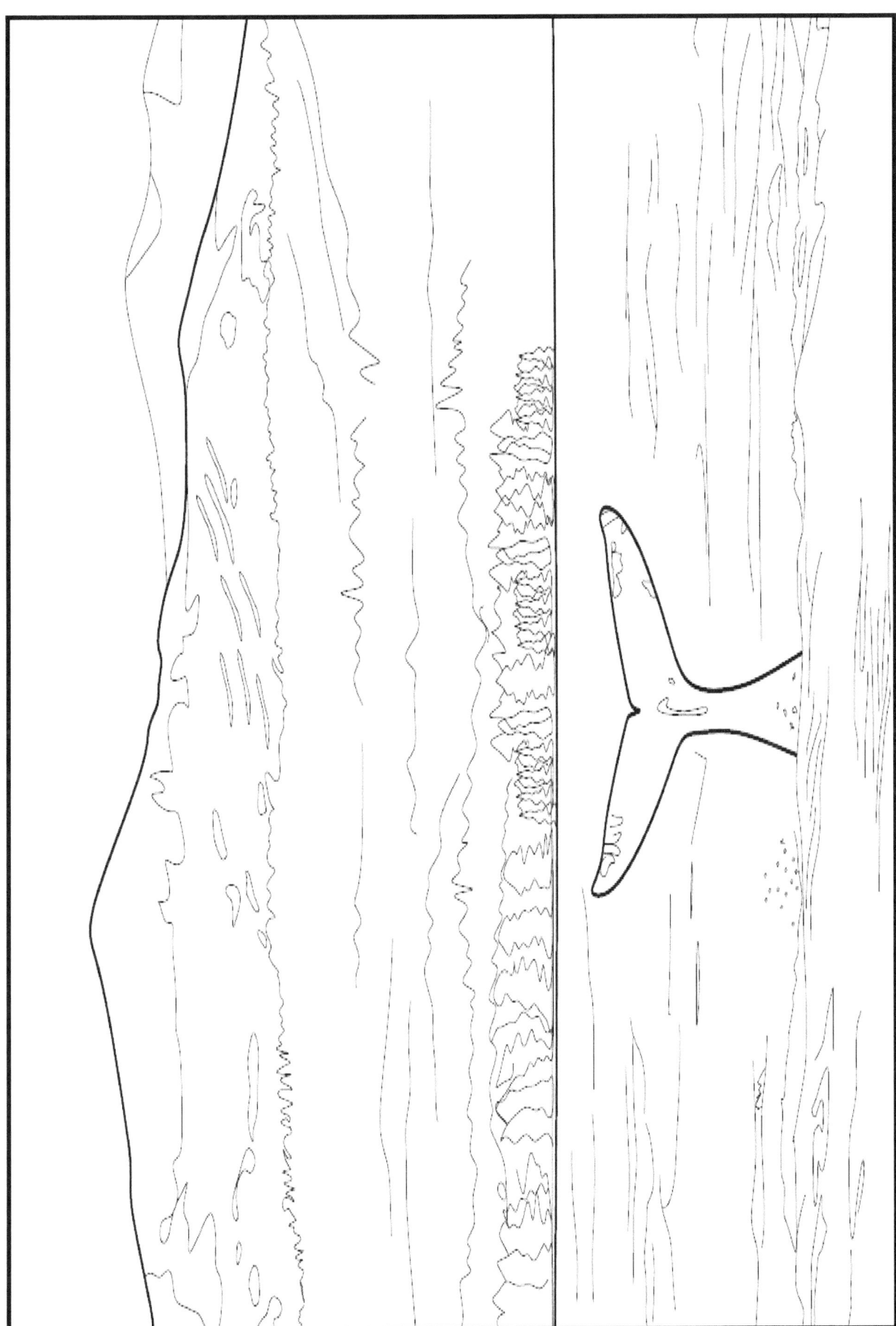

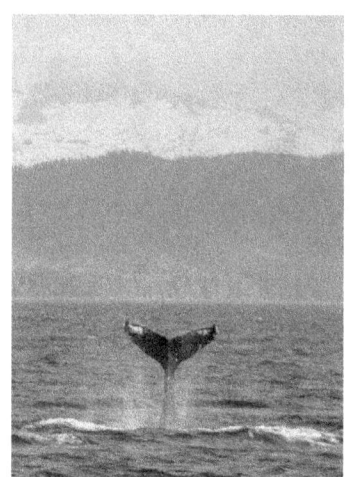

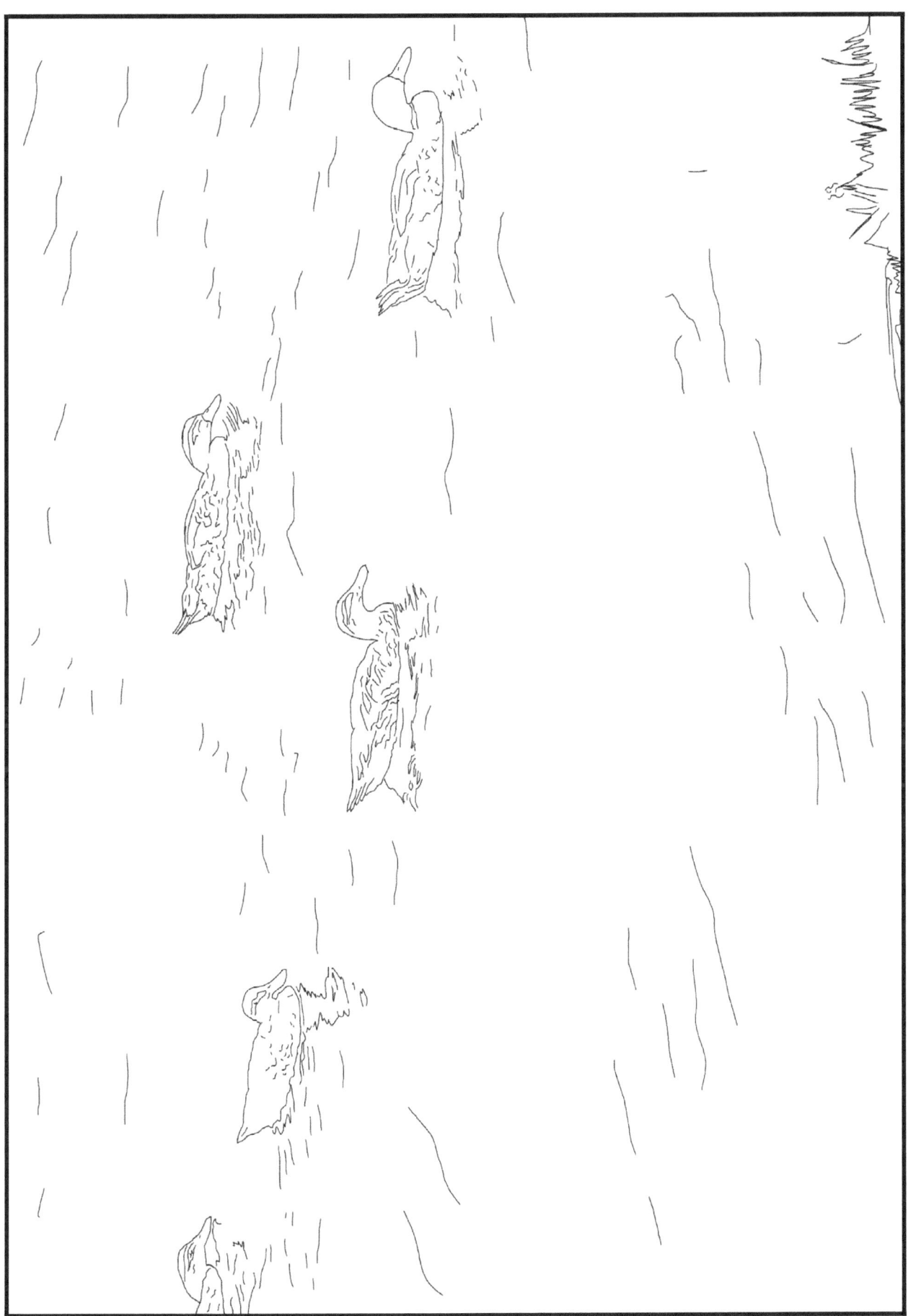

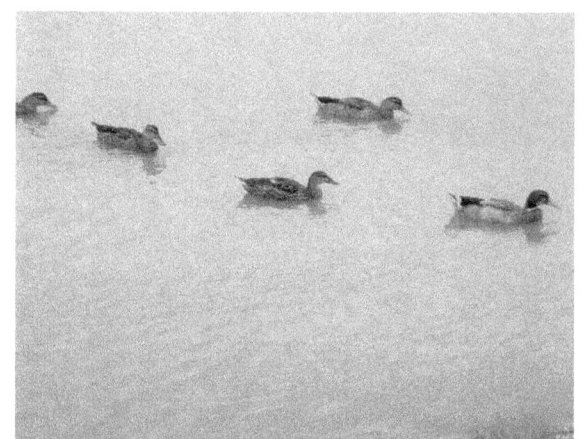

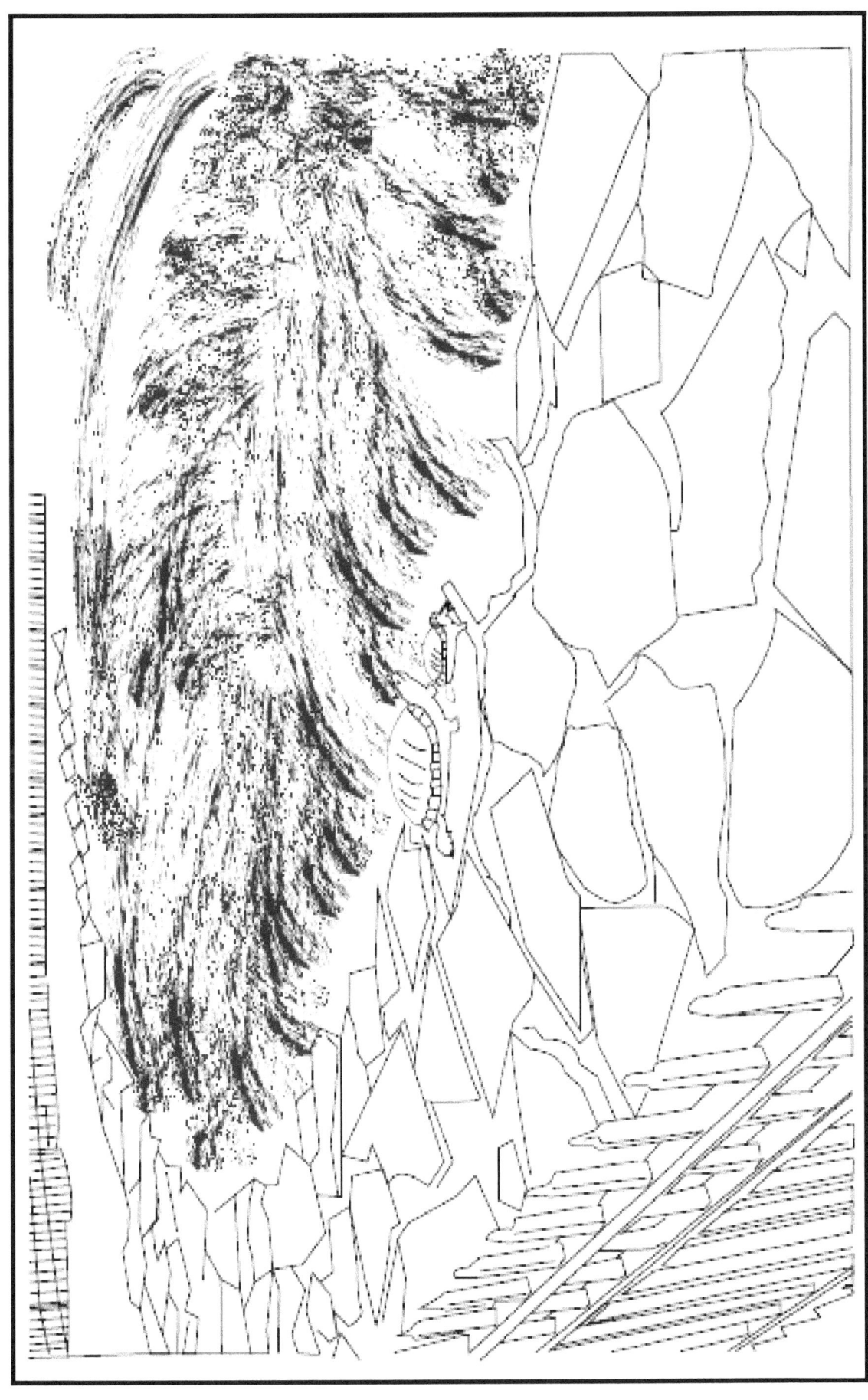

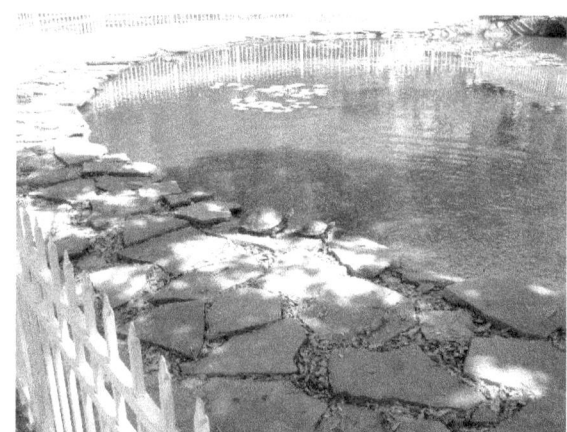

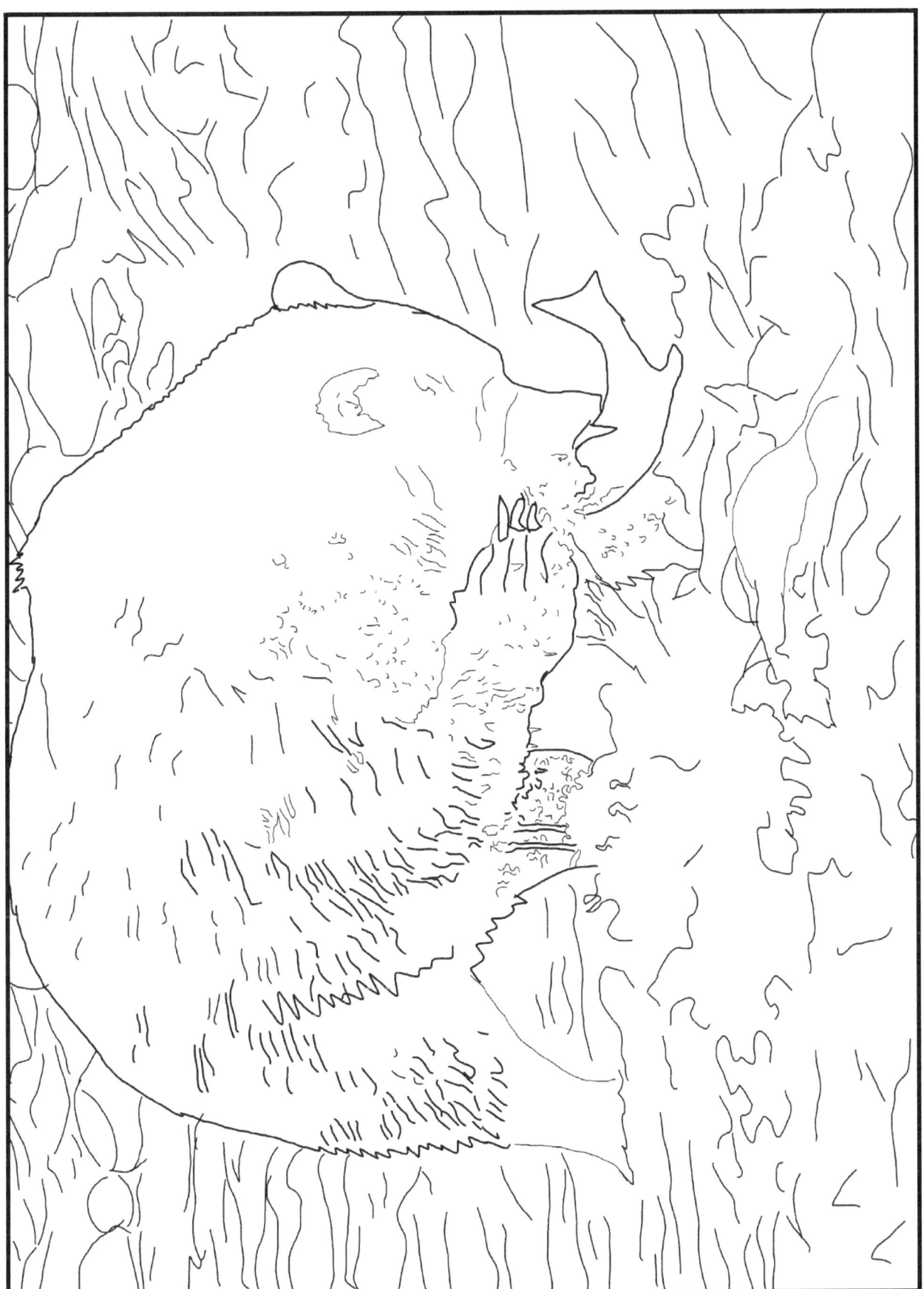

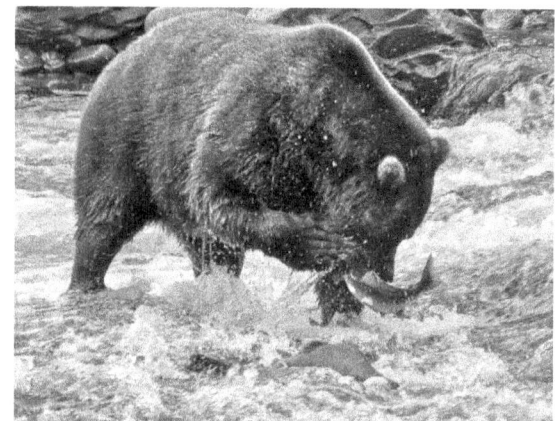

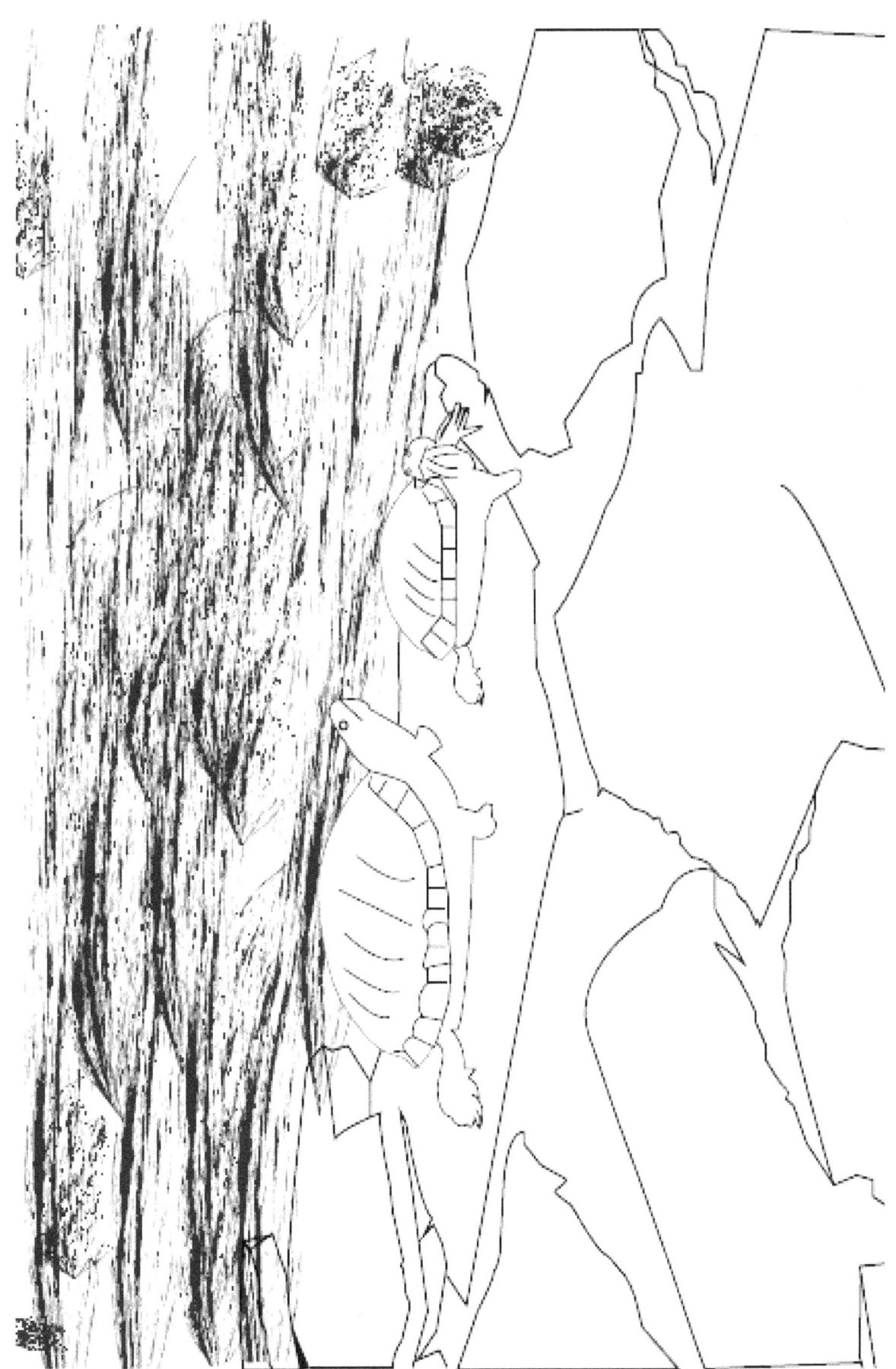

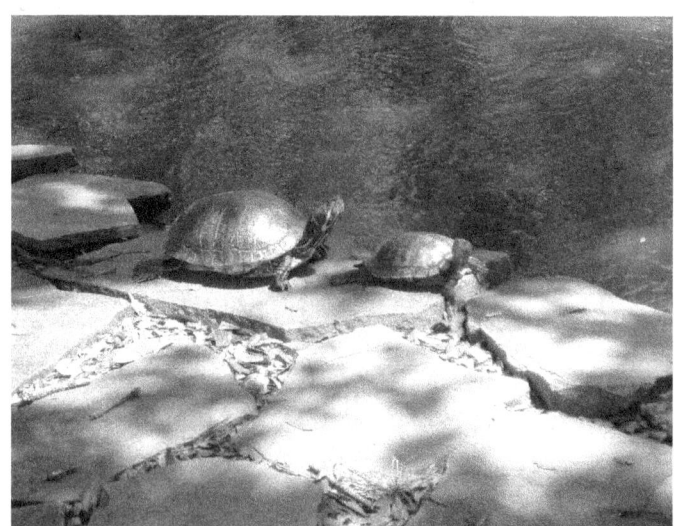

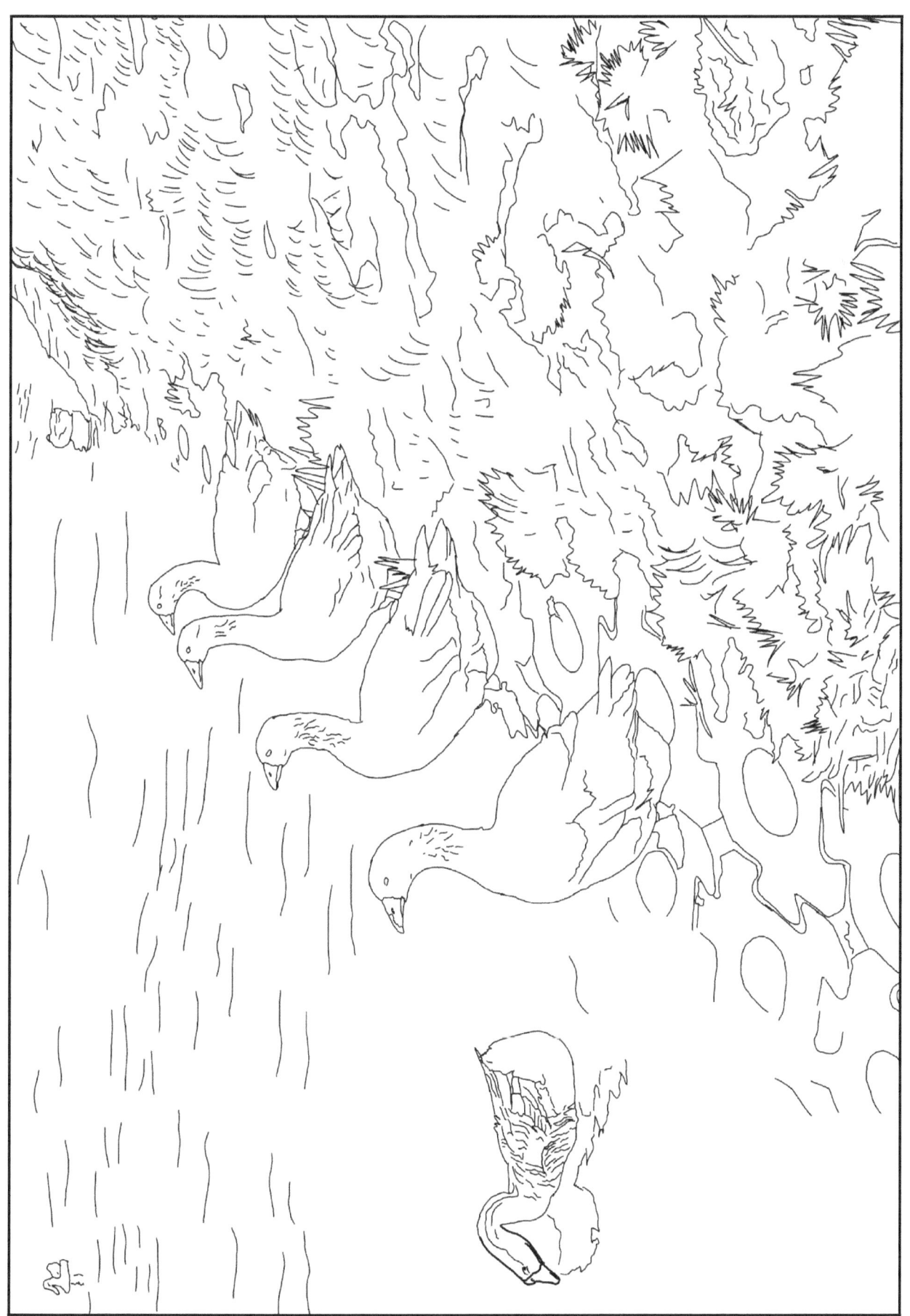

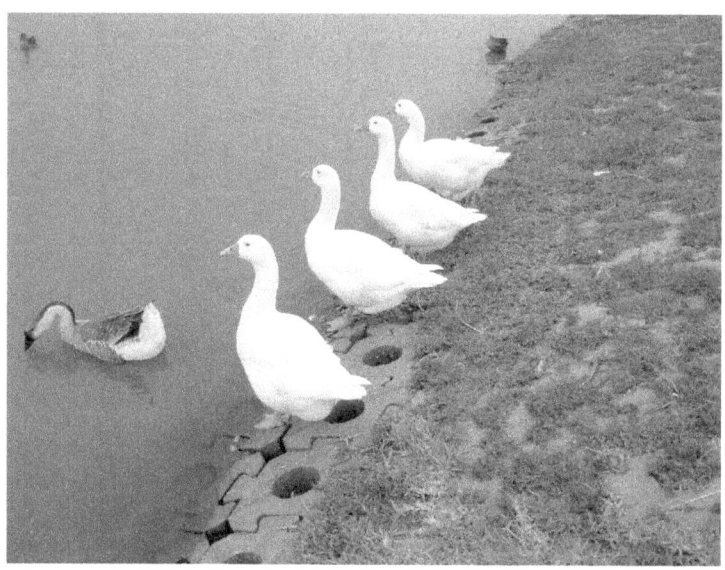

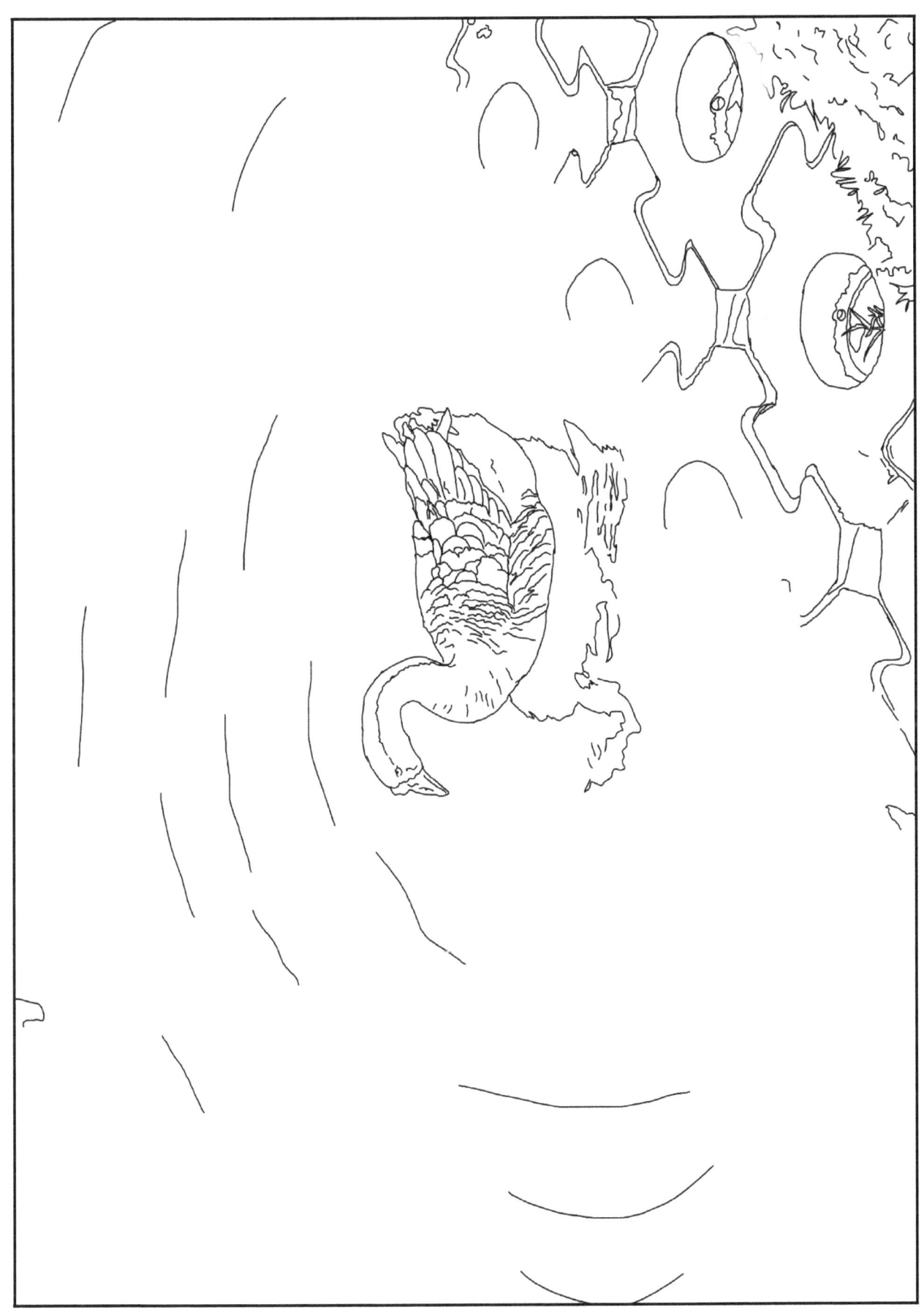

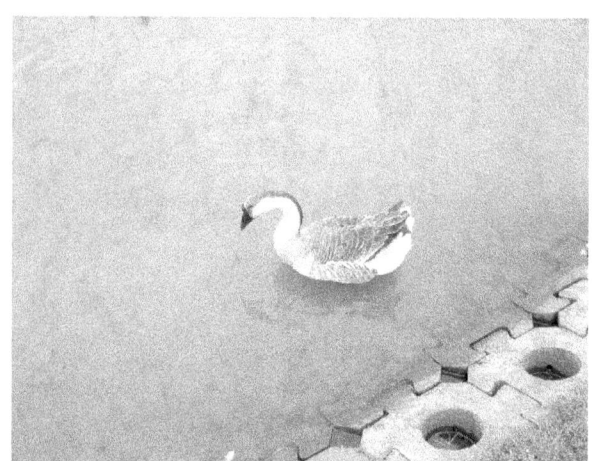

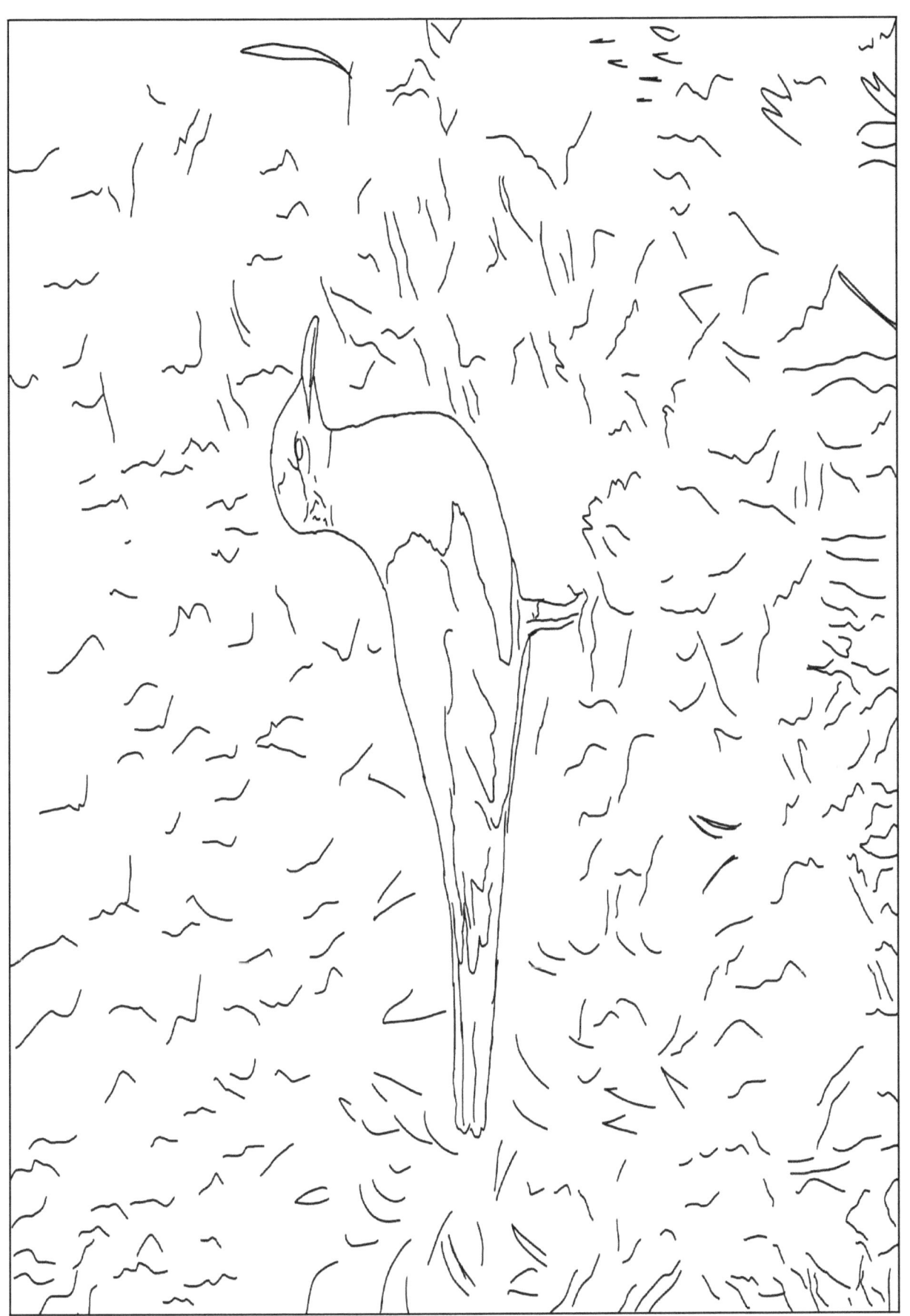

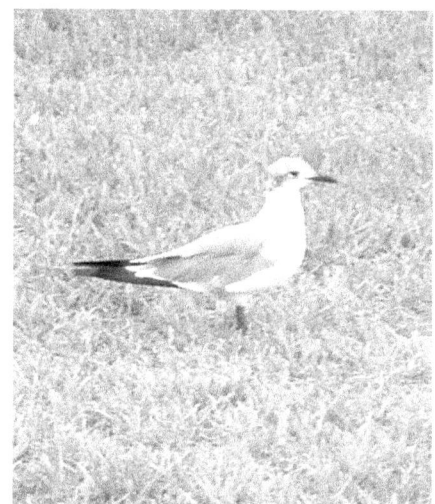

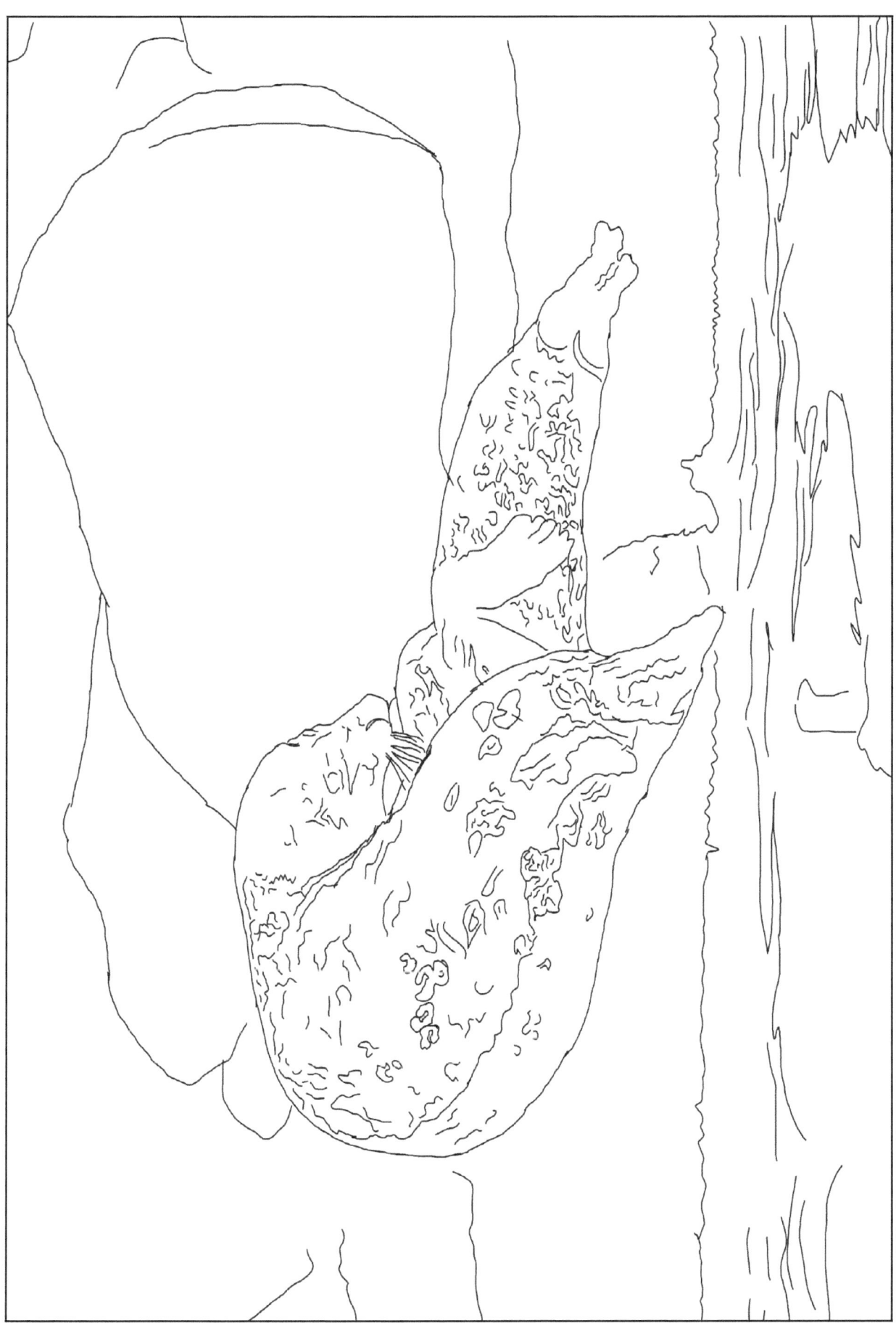

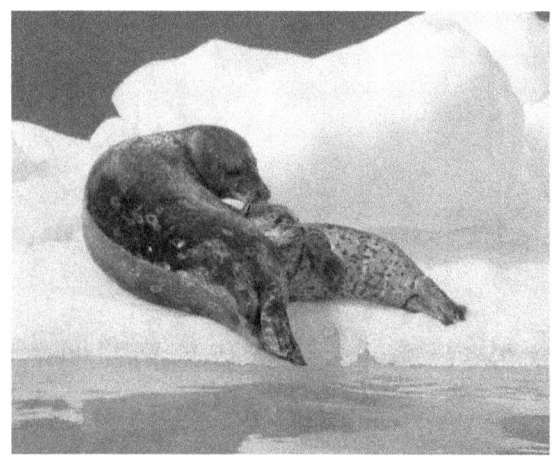

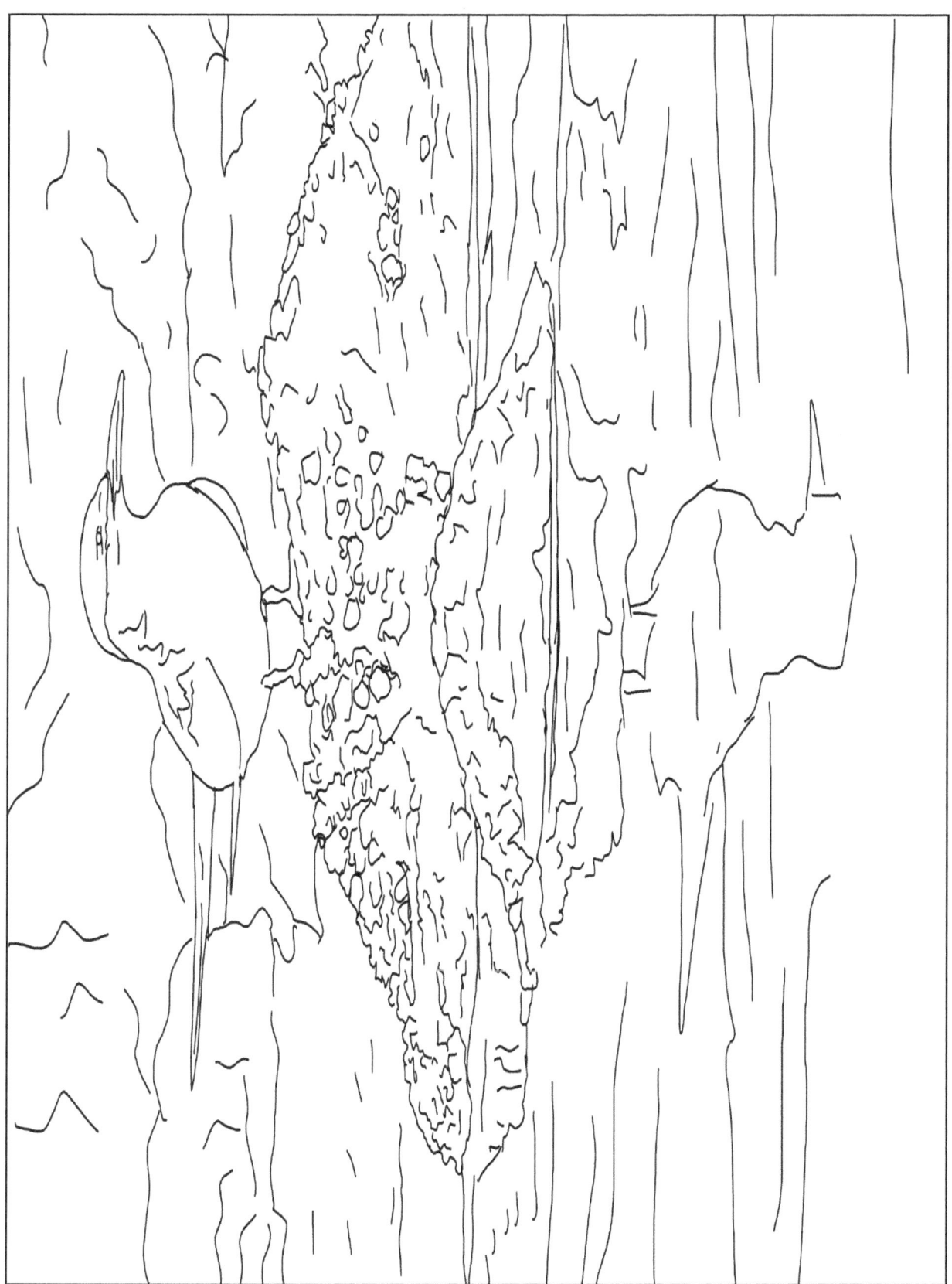

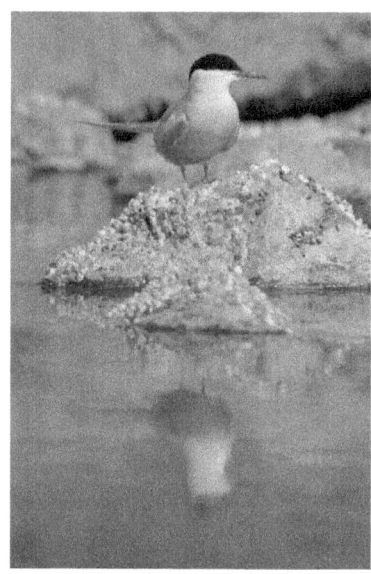

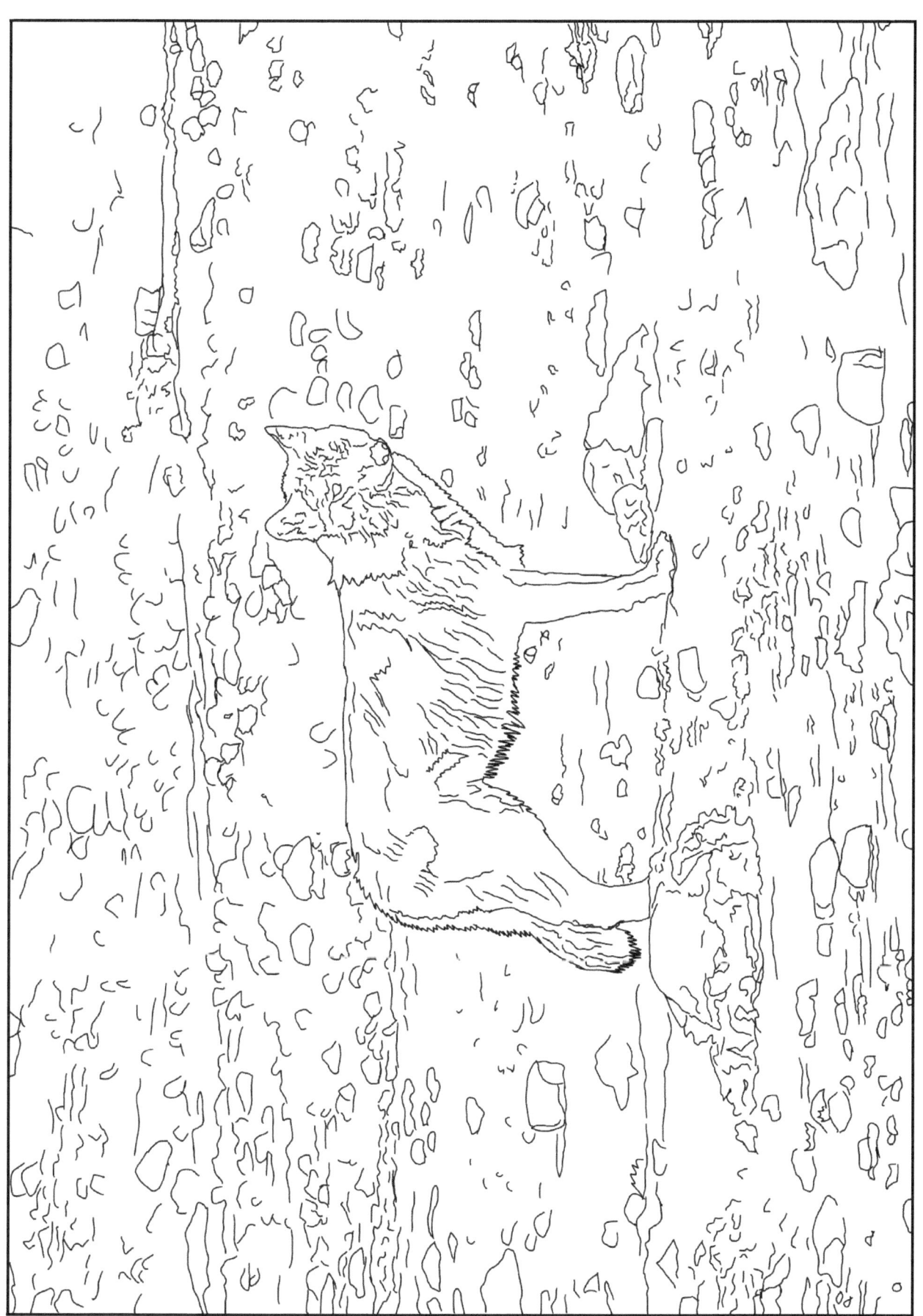

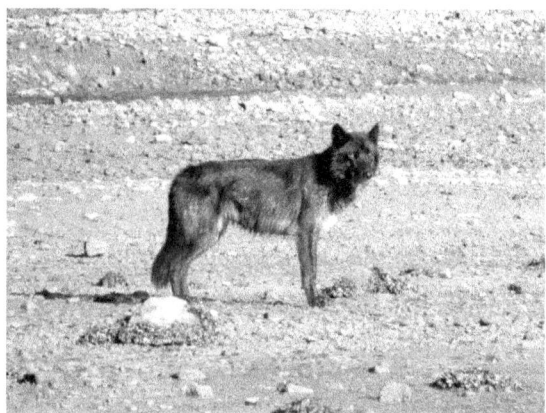

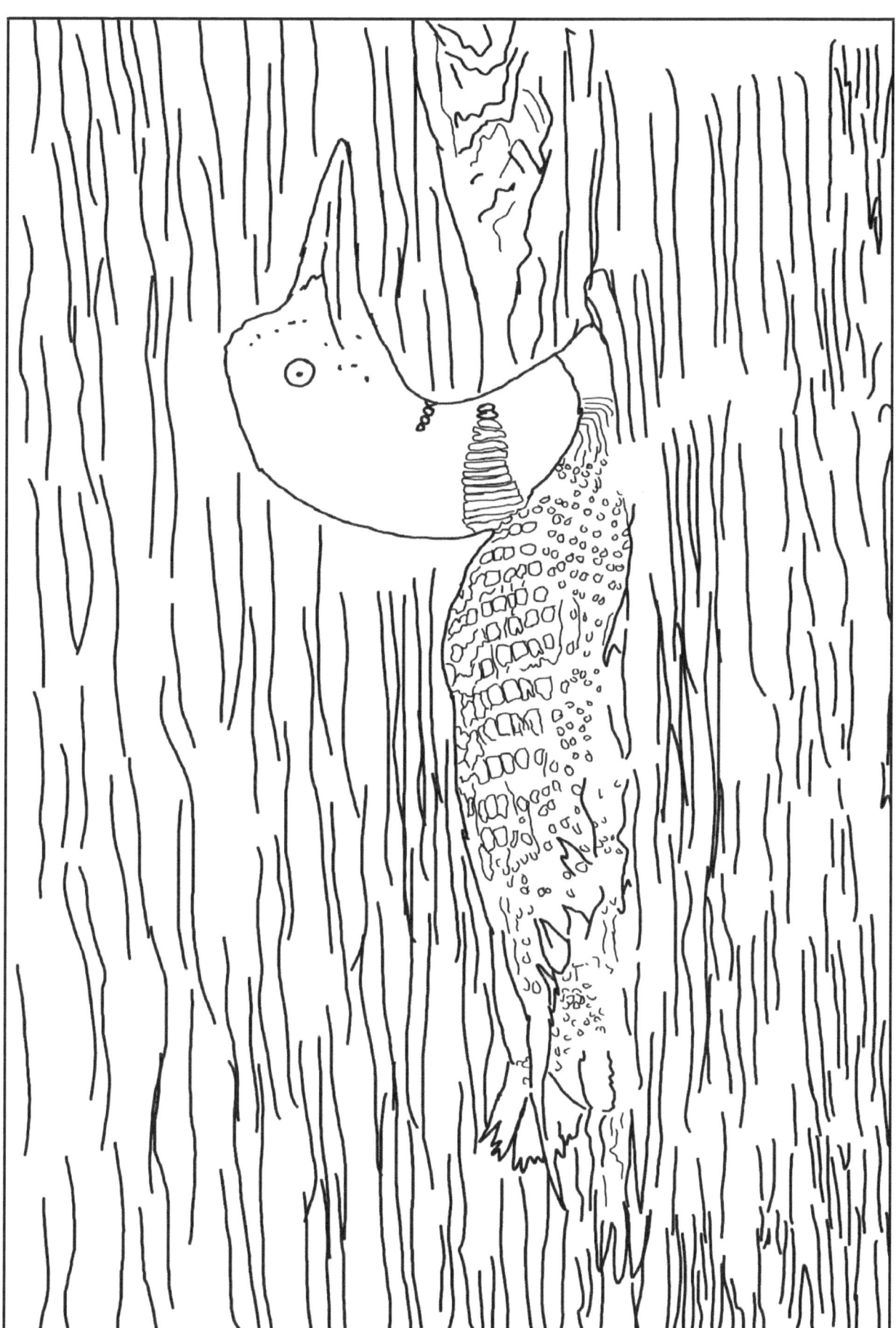

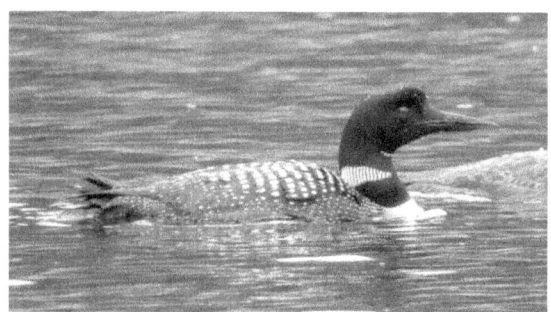

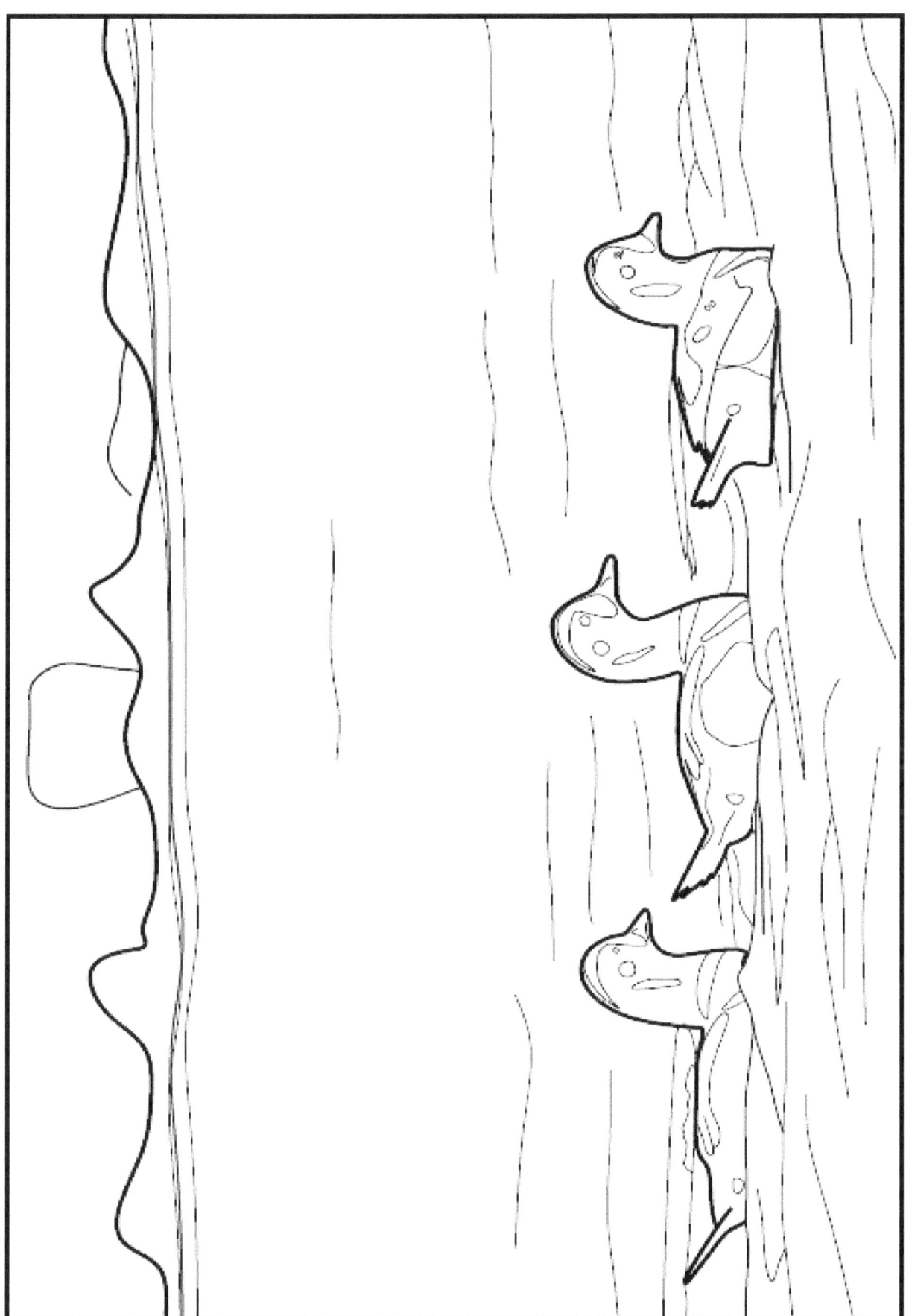

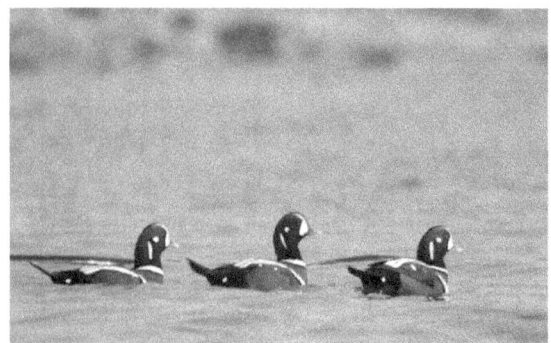

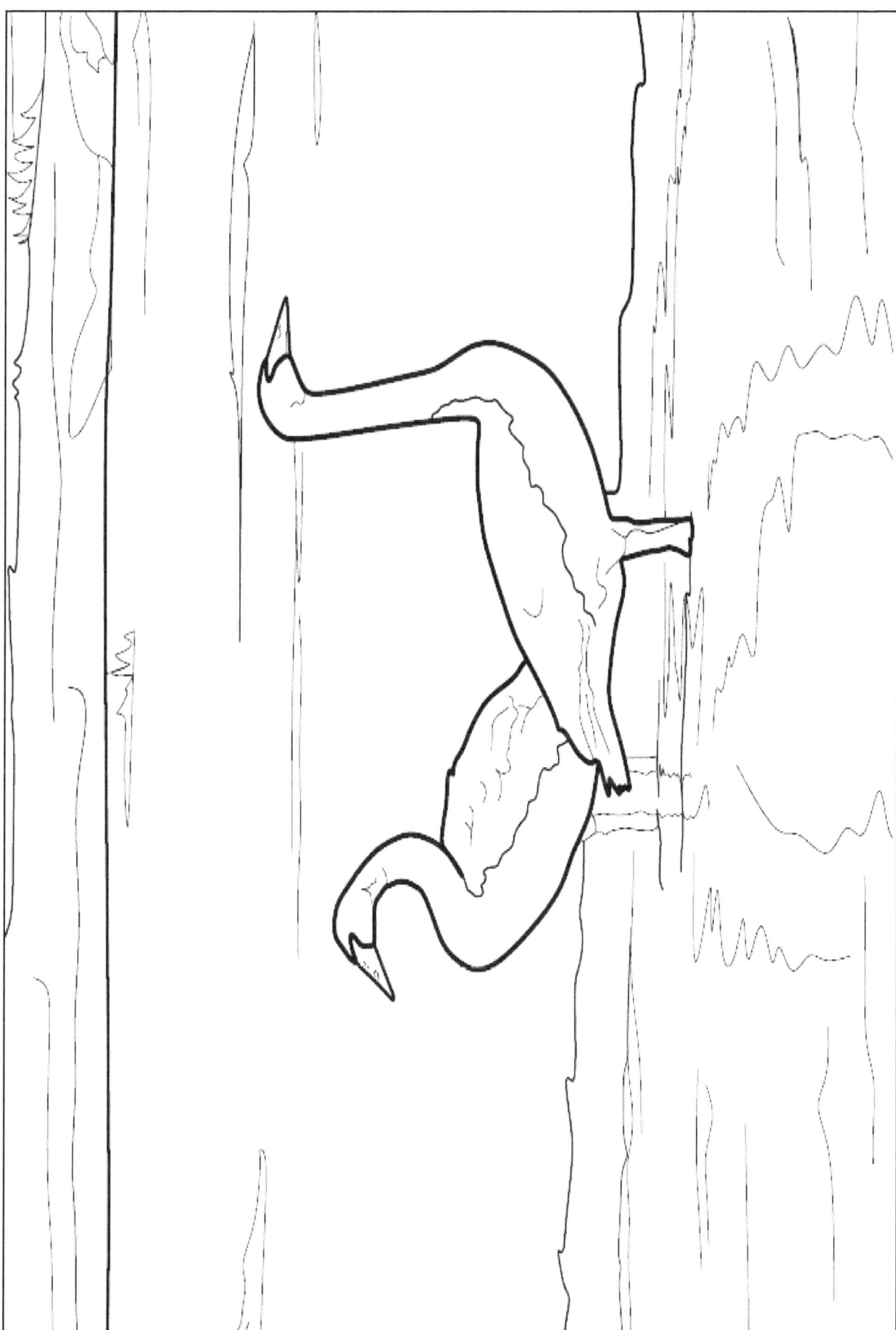

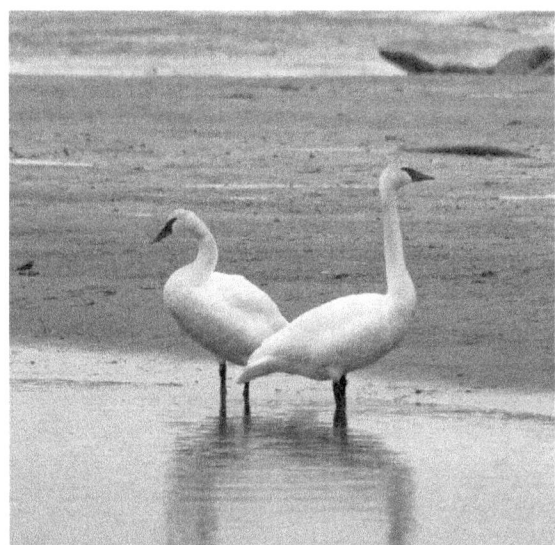

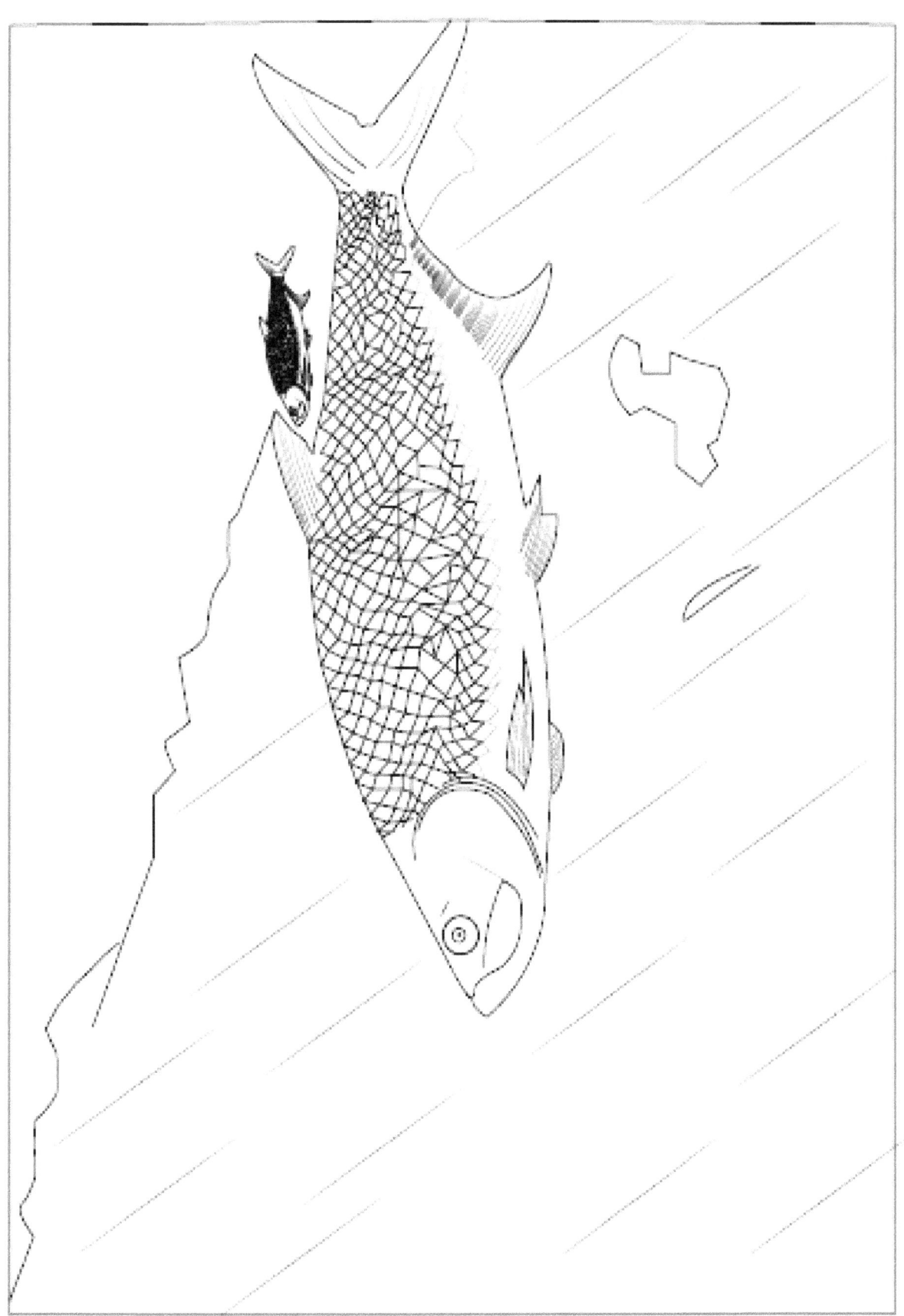

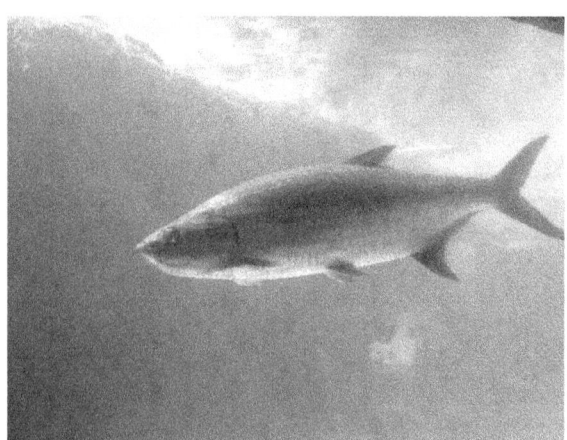

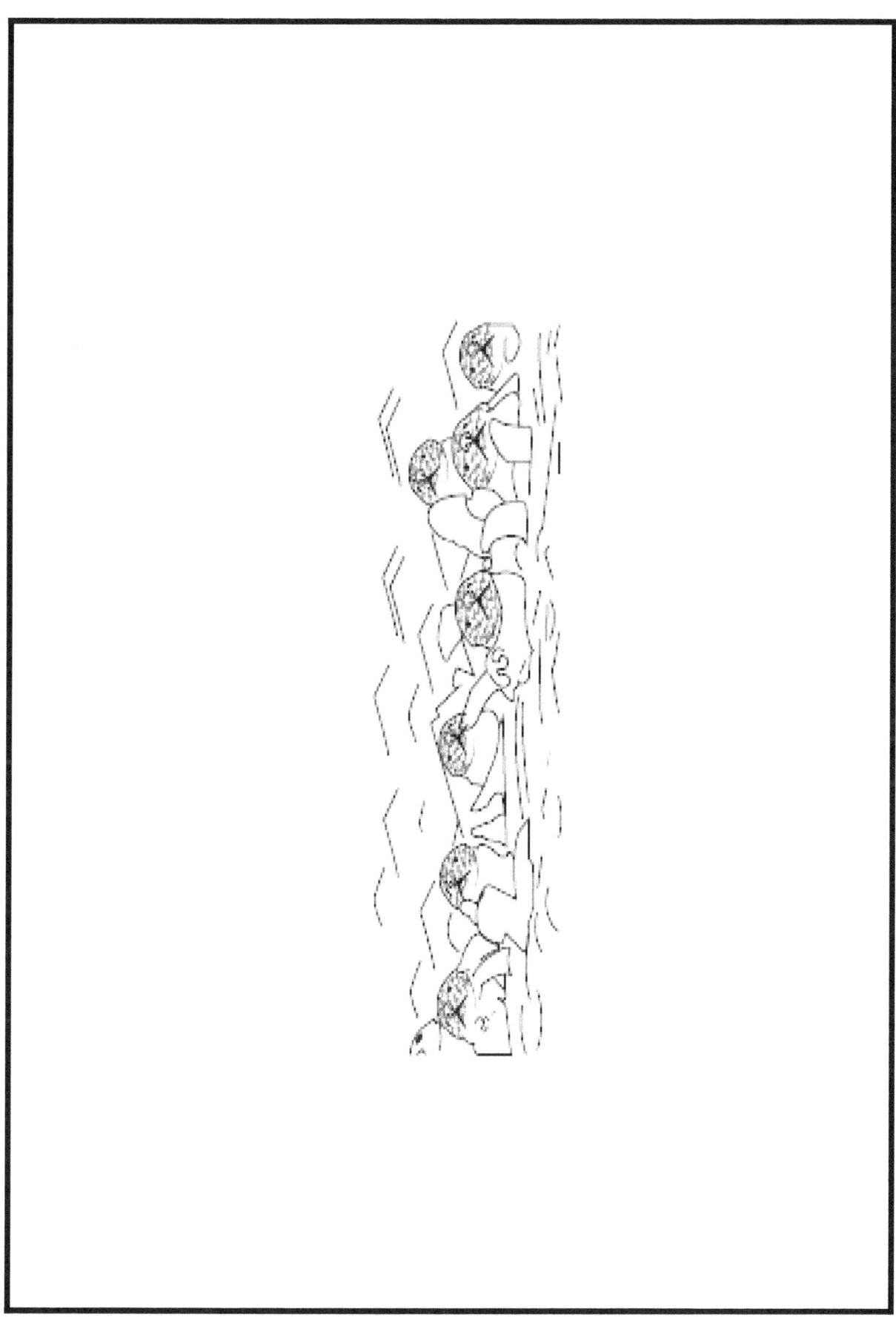

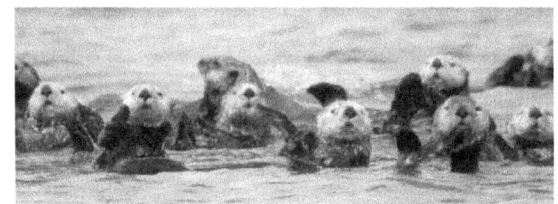

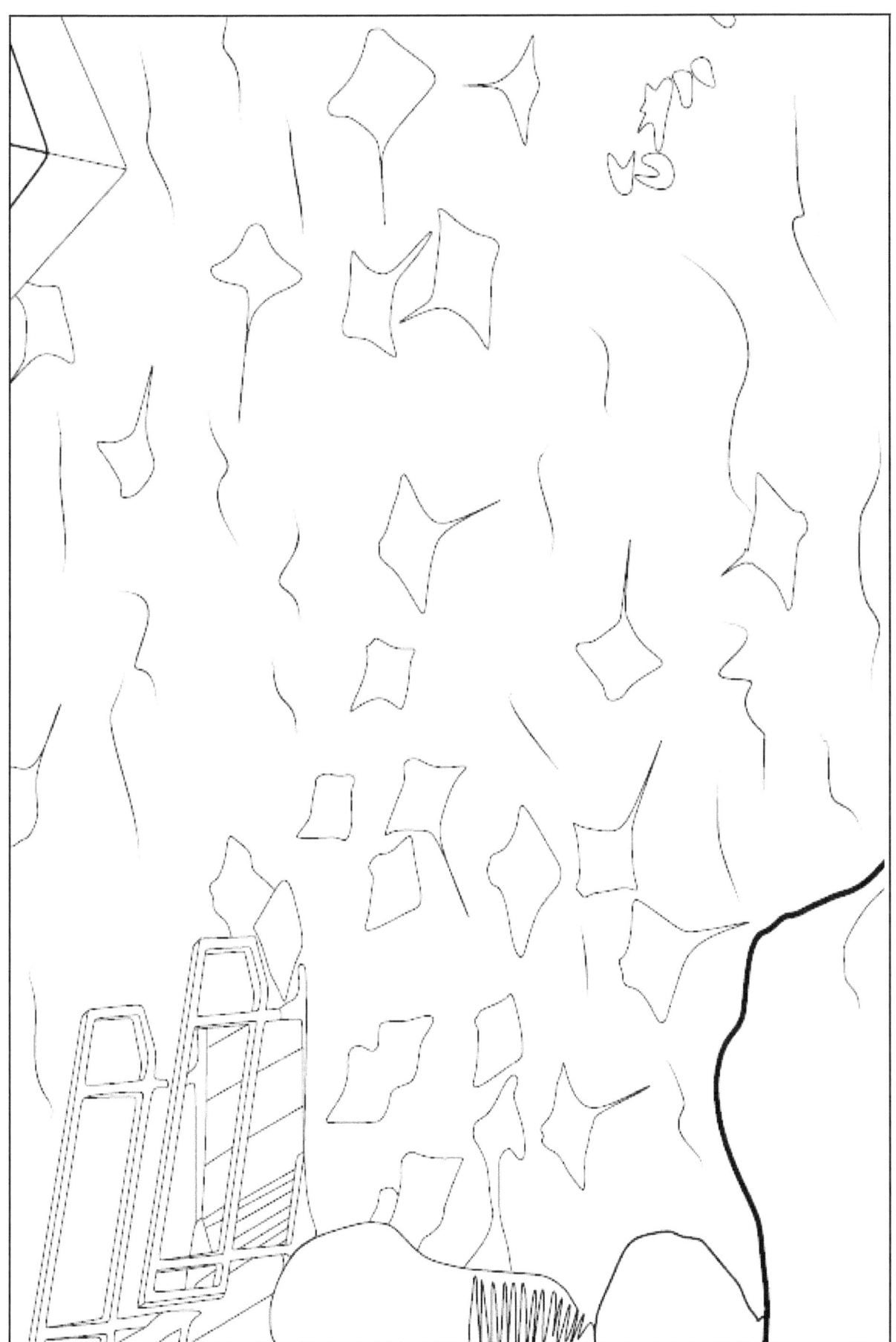

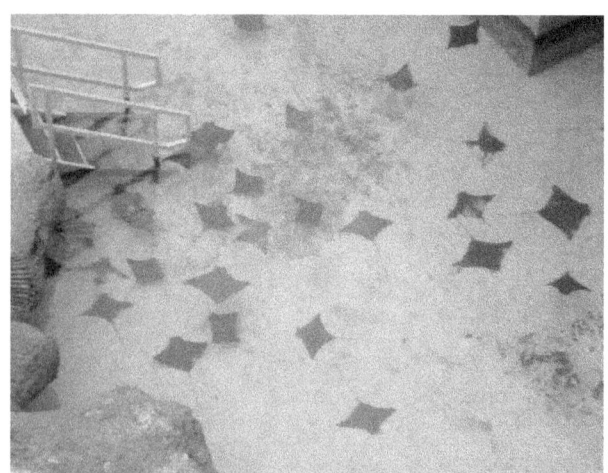

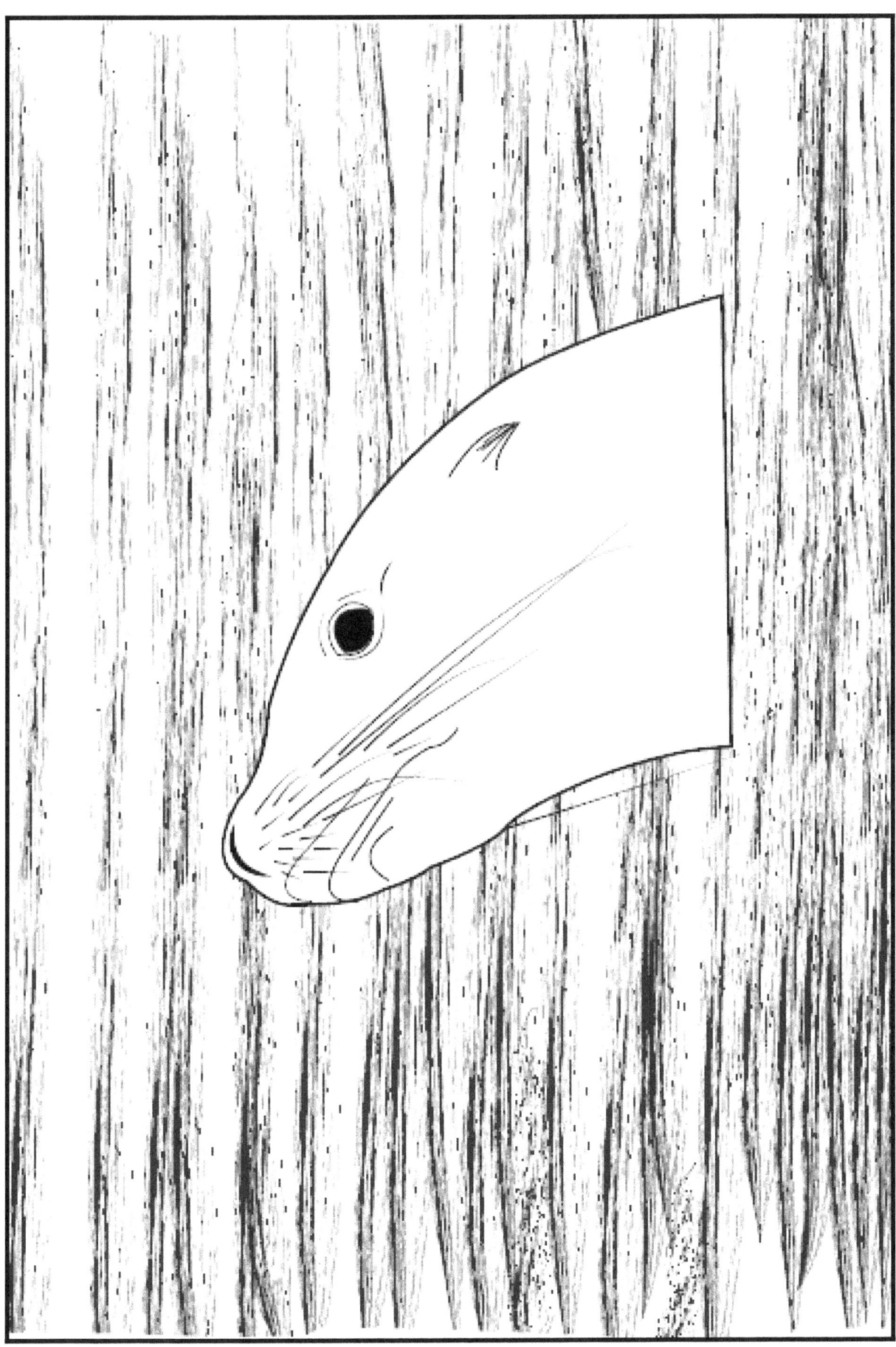

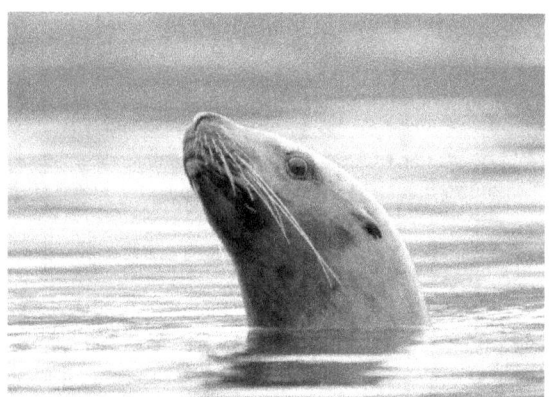

www.ingramcontent.com/pod-product-compliance
Lightning Source LLC
Chambersburg PA
CBHW080441220526
45465CB00007B/2728